Miracles
in
Mexico

Miracles in Mexico

by
James C. Hefley
and
Hugh Steven

MOODY PRESS
CHICAGO

Library of Congress Catalog Card Number: 76-181585
ISBN: 0-8024-5410-0

Printed in the United States of America

Contents

Preface

INTEREST IN MISSIONARY MIRACLES in New Guinea, Amazonia, and the Congo has been so great that we've overlooked dramatic happenings right next door in Mexico.

During nine trips to Mexico (including two summers of residence), I've learned about what God is doing through Wycliffe Bible Translators in the Indian tribes of our neighbor to the south. There are thousands of new believers (fifteen thousand in one tribe alone), and dramatic social and economic advance in almost one hundred tribes. This has been the result of the sacrificial service of over three hundred Wycliffe members, backed by the progressive Mexican government. Descendants of the pyramid-building Aztec and Mayan tribes and many other peoples now can say, "God speaks our languages!"

On my first visit to Mexico, I met Hugh and Norma Steven, Canadian members of Wycliffe, who know and love the nation next to their own homeland. Since then Hugh and I have been writing stories about the "trophies" of Bible translation in Mexico. A dozen appear in this book. In addition, we have included a first chapter that gives a panoramic view of thiry-six years of Wycliffe service.

Hugh, a skilled photographer, has provided a portfolio of pictures (many are his own); and I have organized and edited the final manuscript.

Together, we thank several publishers for their permission to use copyrighted material which appeared in their publications: *Christian Life* for "Miracles in Mexico" (here entitled "The Larger Miracle"); David C. Cook Publishing Company for "Shepherd of the Desert" and "Tarahumara Triumph," which appeared in *Sunday Digest;* Scripture Press Foundation for "The Chamula's Unknown God" and "Domingo and the Fakers"; and World Vision for "The Church in Tomato Gulch," "Tell Us Where God Lives," and "An Aztec Merchant Meets the Master." Several articles appeared in *Christian Times* and other publications, with book rights reserved by the authors.

We are immeasurably indebted to William Cameron Townsend, founder and general director of Wycliffe worldwide; Dr. Frank Robbins, director of Wycliffe's Mexico branch; and dozens of Wycliffe members in Mexico. They shared with us stories from almost forty years of service. We have only "entered into their labors."

For those interested in a deeper understanding of Wycliffe's service in Mexico, we suggest two books:

Manuel by Hugh Steven (Westwood, N.J.: Revell, 1970): Biography of the young Totonac Indian leader whose story is too briefly told in chapter 11.

Peril by Choice by James C. Hefley (Grand Rapids: Zondervan, 1968): Biographies of John and Elaine Beekman, translators to the Chol Indians of southern Mexico.

For those wanting to know more about Mexico's history and development in recent years, I presume to suggest

Aaron Saenz: Mexico's Revolutionary Capitalist by James C. Hefley (Waco: Word, 1970): The modern history of Mexico is viewed through the story of Mexico's greatest living patriot, who is a warm friend of Wycliffe.

J.C.H.

Introduction

IT'S CALLED the United States. The United States of Mexico. Not with fifty states like the United States of America, but with twenty-nine states and two territories.

One territory is the Southern Territory of Baja California—a long, finger-thin peninsula of hot, dry stone and sand that Mexicans call their fleshless arm.

The other is Quintana Roo—a little-known, thinly populated tropical territory of rich hardwoods, jaguars, and heavy humidity. It hangs into the blue-green Carribean on the eastern side of the Yucatan Peninsula like a skier's tassle.

In between and including these two extremes are twenty-nine states that make up one of the most beautiful, exciting, charming, and bewildering countries in the world.

Just over one-fifth the size of the United States and with one-fifth of its population, Mexico has sprinkled its magical cultural dust deep into every crevice of North American life.

Few people realize that the thick slice of tomato

on our hamburgers came first from Mexico and is an Aztec word, as are coyote, avocado, chile, and ocelot. Nor do they know that chocolate, vanilla, and chicle resin for our chewing gum all came from Mexico and were used by ancient Mayans a thousand years before Christ.

Mexican art, architecture, language, ceramics, food, music, and romance are almost as much a part of our American way of life as they are Mexican. Yet, with all its pre- and post- Colombian influence, Mexico still remains a mystery to most of the tourists who ebb and flow across the thin 2,000-mile Mexican-United States border.

Born with spectacular volcanic violence, the rugged Sierra Madre Mountains form a giant V along Mexico's western and eastern flanks. This geological catastrophe covers almost two-thirds of Mexico's land mass. Time, water and wind have since softened many of the exquisite cones, so that Mount Orizaba, Mexico's highest peak at 18,696 feet, is more symmetrical and delicate than Japan's Fujiyama. The Aztecs call this near perfect cone, "Citlaltepetl," mountain of the star.

The uniqueness of Mexico is not just being able in a day's drive to leave the snowfields of Orizaba for a swim in tropical Acapulco Bay. Or that the University of Mexico, founded in 1551, is the oldest university in the Americas—or—or—or—we could go on for many more pages! But the striking and most mysterious phenomena to outsiders, and most important to the Wycliffe Bible Translators, are Mexico's Indian peoples.

Someone said of Mexico that she has been ruled by Spain, converted by Rome, governed by Austria under French auspices, exploited by England and Germany, overwhelmed by the United States, confused by European intellectualism, and wooed by Russia. Yet she remains what she always was—Indian.

Of the current 48 million people, over 10 percent are pure aboriginal and 60 percent mestizo. It was the Zapotec Indians who took a mountain apart and put it back together to create the flat-top pyramids and tombs of Monte Albán. It was the copper-skinned, obsidian-eyed Mayans who, in the jungle state of Chiapas, raised the towering monuments of Palenque and Bonampak.

But the clever Indian minds that worked brilliantly in astronomy, calendar-making, engineering, and mathematics were unable to live peacefully as neighbors. The bloodthirsty gods that many tribes worshiped demanded sacrifices that only war could satisfy.

By A.D. 1000 most of the astonishing cities and high civilizations that marked Mexico's golden age were covered with dust, sand, and jungle vegetation. All had fallen to wars, epidemics, and an overstrained agricultural economy that forced scattered migrations.

In the four centuries following the conquest, millions of Indians were branded, maimed, and killed. Almost three hundred tribal groups dwindled to what was once thought to be about fifty-five. In spite of this, the Indian has endured. Today, through scientific investigation, Wycliffe has discovered over 120 distinctly different language groups.

Mexico's boldest leaders in the century and a half since independence have been Indian or leaders of Indians. José Maria Morelos was a military genius and one of the most heroic figures in the war for independence. Benito Juárez, the Lincolnesque leader of the reform movement and president of Mexico, was a full-blooded Zapotec. Porfirio Díaz, who ruled Mexico for thirty-three years, was Mixtec.

Yet, for all her great heroes, most of Mexico's Indians remain unchanged and as varied as her landscape. They can be lean, sinewy, and eagle-faced like the northern Tarahumaras, or short, plump and moon-faced like the Popolucas of Veracruz. They can be good-natured, indolent, somber or compulsive. In the central highlands, women are modest and heavily shrouded. In Mixtec country they are blouseless. Zapotec women from the mountains are silent and reserved. Those from the Isthmus of Tehuantepec are bold, beautiful, and vain.

In spite of these differences, most of Mexico's Indians have language, social, and geographic separation in common. The inhabitants of some areas have never seen an American, gasoline motor, or electric light bulb. They do not understand or speak Spanish, Mexico's national language.

It was for this reason that Wycliffe Bible Translators, with a fresh God-given sparkle of faith, came to Mexico thirty-five years ago. The first ten Mexico branch members believed then, as do the current three hundred, that no matter how isolated or small, each language group should have the Scriptures in their language.

Today, through Bible translation, evangelism, and church-planting, that dream is becoming a reality. The Mexico branch publications staff of computer operators, printers, artists, typists, layout people, and supervisors often works a twelve to fifteen-hour day preparing and publishing the increasing flow of translated Scriptures and Testaments.

Of the 101 language groups occupied, 86 have some portion of Scripture. Fourteen New Testaments have been published, and twelve are in the process of being printed. Believers range from the ones and twos in recently occupied tribes to over eight to ten thousand among the Chols and Tzeltals.

In the following stories you will experience the growth, struggles, joys, and sorrows of some of Mexico's outstanding Indian believers. In lush green, mist-filled valleys of Oaxaca, on sandy beaches of Mexico's northwest mainland coast, and in desert and jungle huts, Indians are being reborn. Not with the violence of a volcanic eruption, but with the steady illuminating brilliance of God's translated message of hope and life.

H.S.

1

The Larger Miracle

DULL SUNLIGHT seeped through the morning haze that draped the oldest city of North America. On this "Day of the Indian," April 19, hundreds of the first Mexicans were burning their cornfields around the mountains that encircled mile-and-a-half high Mexico City—a method of destructive agriculture followed for millenia. The smoke from brush fires blended with fumes from hundreds of factories in the metropolitan area of seven million, climbed over the twin snow-clad peaks that rise above the great mountain bowl where the bejeweled Aztec kingdom flourished five centuries ago.

I glanced up at the four-story mosaic on the facade of the Wycliffe Bible Translators' new study center. The mosaic mural pictured the ancient Aztec torch runner as a symbol of hope for primitive Indians now rising from poverty and illiteracy. I thought of the difference between their Spanish conqueror, Hernan Cortez, and the short, freckled Californian at the door. The Spaniard had come with soldiers, greedy

17

for gold and conquest. Over four centuries later,
Townsend, weak from illness and with a sick wife,
had crossed the northern border to give Mexico's
Indians the treasures of the gospel. Mexico has no
monuments to Cortez, whose bones are interred a
short drive from Wycliffe headquarters. There will
certainly be honored memorials to Cameron Townsend after the translator's death.

Well-dressed Mexican visitors were now stepping
from taxis and chauffered cars and entering the building between an honor guard of some sixty Aztec girls
in colorful red sweaters and white skirts. At the entrance Cameron Townsend, Wycliffe's founder and
general director who had recently returned from
surveying minority languages in Russia, was shaking
hands and giving repeated *abrazo* embraces to old
friends—government cabinet members, educators,
professors, and other distinguished Mexican friends
of Wycliffe.

Inside the painted stone-walled auditorium the ceremony of dedication began. A parade of Indian musi-
cians from various tribes entertained the overflow
crowd with music and folk dances kept alive since
preconquest days. Mexican educators gave flowery
orations to Wycliffe's linguistic and literacy service
to the country's four million Indians. Dr. Mauricio
Magdaleno, a prominent writer, recalled, "Once we
saw Indians as a burden, even a disease, but now we
see them as a great treasure of strength for national
development."

But Cameron Townsend drew the warmest applause for saying, "Mexico is mother to all our work. Almost five hundred tribes in Vietnam, Nepal, and eighteen other countries are coming into the light because of what happened here."

From previous research on a Wycliffe missionary documentary[1], I had learned how Wycliffe's worldwide ministry had been born and shaped in Mexico in the spirit of Townsend's life motto: "Ourselves your servants for Jesus' sake."[2]

Townsend set his sights on Mexico three years after returning from fourteen years in Guatemala where he had set the pattern for modern translation methods by giving the New Testament to 200,000 illiterate Cakchiquel Indians and teaching them to read it. Still weak from a bout with tuberculosis, he and L. L. Legters crossed the muddy Rio Grande in 1933. Legters, a veteran missionary explorer, shared Townsend's burden for the Bibleless tribes, then thought to number only a few hundred. Mrs. Townsend suffered from a heart ailment and stayed behind.

Mexican officials stopped them cold at the border. The country was caught up in a wave of anticlericalism, resulting from a power struggle between the government and the Catholic hierarchy. Religious workers were not wanted.

As they waited and hoped for a miracle, Townsend

1. James C. Hefley, *Peril By Choice* (Grand Rapids: Zondervan, 1968).
2. Second Corinthians 4:5.

remembered a Mexican educator who had visited him years before in Guatemala. He'd been impressed with the Cakchiquel translation and literacy program. He later wrote to Townsend, "You should do this for my country's Indians." Townsend began digging through a briefcase for the yellowed letter.

"Here it is!" Townsend suddenly shouted. "The letter from the educator, Dr. Moises Saenz."

He passed it to the customs men. They knew about Saenz, founder of the high school system in Mexico. But they had orders not to permit "religious racketeers" across the border. What to do? Call Mexico City for instructions.

Finally they could enter, but Legters was not to preach, nor Townsend to study any Indian languages. But once in the capital, they made friends with a socialist professor and a high official, an atheist, who helped them get permission for a language survey.

The survey turned up what they had expected: Mexico's Indians were locked in poverty and illiteracy because Spanish was a foreign tongue. Townsend and Legters offered to help the new breed of reform-minded Mexican educators bring the Indians into the light of civilized day. Then Townsend received news that his wife was gravely ill back in California. "We'll be back," he told Mexican officials, "with more workers." The officials sent sympathies to Mrs. Townsend but were noncommittal about permitting work with the Indians. One frankly said, "The Indians have too much religion already."

Townsend took his sick wife to the Arkansas Ozarks where her health took a turn for the better. Then he and Legters scoured the country for recruits. In 1934 they opened a linguistic training school, called Camp Wycliffe, in an abandoned farmhouse near Sulphur Springs, Arkansas, with two students.

Two years later religious persecution eased in Mexico, although foreign religious workers were still unwanted. Townsend traded a washing machine for a trailer, helped his still-ailing wife and niece Evelyn Griset (who went along to care for Mrs. Townsend) into an old Buick that burned a quart of oil every twenty miles, and started again for the border.

The customs men looked in amazement at the sight of the tandem monster lumbering toward them. "What a grand *coche* (car) and *casa* (house)!" one shouted in admiration.

Townsend stopped the old Buick and handed an envelope of documents to the chief. "We're coming to translate the Bible into Aztec and to teach the Indians how to read and write," he told the customs man.

"Good," he nodded, giving the papers only a cursory once-over. "Our poor Indians need help. Proceed, Señor."

Road construction delayed them a week a few miles down the road. Further on, the car almost skidded over a high precipice; only the weight of the old trailer kept it balanced until a steam-shovel operator came to the rescue.

Finally they reached the northern edge of the capital, where Townsend stopped to fix the trailer's taillight. Suddenly two police motorcycles roared up beside him. One policeman looked at the license and smiled. "Señor, we visited California last year and were given the courtesies by the Los Angeles chief of police. Let us escort you through traffic."

With sirens screaming in front and behind, the old Buick and trailer groaned through city traffic. The next morning they stopped in the dirt plaza of the Aztec village of Tetelcingo, where Townsend hoped to translate the first Aztec New Testament.

On one side of the plaza they noticed a strange stone church. Above the doorway was a cross and a painted sun, the symbol of Aztec worship. The Indians had fused their own religion with the Catholicism imported by the Spaniards.

Townsend greeted the village mayor in Spanish and asked, "Señor, how do you say *buenos días* in your Aztec language?"

"Panultijtzino," replied the perplexed Indian.

Townsend turned to the crowd that had gathered, bowed and said, *"Panultijtzino."* Then he reached for a notebook and exclaimed, "I must write that word down. Tell me another, Señor Mayor."

Soon the mayor was saying, "We thank you, Professor, for speaking our humble language. No man with learning has ever shown interest in us or our poor language before."

Townsend then explained that he not only wanted

to learn the language, but to translate "the supreme God's writings" into Aztec. Would the mayor be his language helper and could he have permission to plant a garden in the plaza? The mayor nodded his head approvingly.

Townsend built a cornstalk fence to keep out the pigs and then planted radishes, lettuce and other vegetables. The poor villagers ate only tortillas and chili peppers, and a few enjoyed beans. One fine day, the "professor" gave out heads of lettuce and radishes with instructions on how to eat them.

Aware that Mexican revolutionary political leaders believed religion "to be the opiate of the masses, and that religious workers were parasites," he had more than horticulture in mind in expanding the Aztec's diet. At his direction, men carried manure into the square and spaded up the ground. He irrigated with waste water from the plaza cistern. When the Aztecs saw water running uphill through the siphon, they cowered in fear, believing the professor was in partnership with the devil. But after he showed them how to do the trick, their fears subsided.

Next came a park with fruit trees, roses, and beds of lettuce, radishes, carrots, beans, and celery. Townsend, his wife, and niece rejoiced as the once-barren and dusty plaza budded and bloomed as Indians came for seeds and plants to start their own gardens. But they were happiest about the conversion of the mayor. He quit beating his twenty-eighth wife, stopped drinking, and, with the professor's help, began translating

Spanish Bible verses into Aztec for village elders.

One warm January day in 1936, Townsend was in work clothes and plucking a chicken for lunch when he heard motors and an unusually large crowd running toward the nearby school. Stepping around to see who had come, he gasped at the sight of President Lazaro Cardenas.

He brushed dirt from his hands and smiled. "Buenos días, Señor Presidente."

The president saw him and smiled back. "Buenos días, Señor Townsend."

Suddenly Townsend realized that President Cardenas had come to see him! The president looked at Townsend's language notes and the park and garden. He grinned in grateful approval when told about the reading classes being conducted in Aztec.

"With your approval, Señor Presidente," Townsend said, "we could bring in other young people to help Mexico's Indians come into the light of learning. For our part, we would want only to translate the Bible."

Cardenas pumped Townsend's hand vigorously. "Of course. Of course. This is just what Mexico needs. Bring in all who wish to come."

A week after Cardenas' visit, a truckload of fruit trees rolled into Tetelcingo. A shipment of livestock followed, then technicians to help the Indians with agriculture. Laundry units were installed in the plaza for village women who had always washed clothes on flat rocks. A large orange grove was planted. Electric lights, a mill for grinding tortillas, a sewing machine, a chil-

dren's playground, and a new school were other bless-
ings that came to Telecingo as a result of the president's visit.

With favor from President Cardenas, new linguists
began trickling into the country to occupy other
tribes. Most had been recruited by Legters who had
stayed behind to raise support and search for new
workers.

Ken and Eunice Pike (brother and sister) and Eugene Nida were among the first recruits. Drs. Pike
and Nida have since become world famous in their
respective fields of linguistics and Bible translation.
Eunice Pike and her partner Florence Hansen became
the first two Wycliffe single girls to go to a tribe.
Before going, Townsend asked them if they were afraid
to go by muleback where no missionary had ever
gone. "Won't God take care of us?" was the reply.
Townsend allowed that God would.

As more new tribes were entered and unwritten
languages deciphered, Wycliffe's policies destined to
be tested worldwide began evolving:

1. *Translate the Bible on a nonsectarian basis.*
This meant, according to Townsend, providing Scripture in native languages to all groups striving to pro-
mote the spiritual welfare of the Indians.

2. *Follow the linguistic approach* by working in the
"language of the soul" which the tribesman under-
stands. "When he learns to read in his ancestral
tongue," Townsend reasoned, "then he can easily
learn the national language."

3. *Serve everyone.* Townsend said, "We serve the Indians by doing for them what has never been done—putting their language into writing and translating the Bible. We serve the governments by teaching the Indians to read and helping them become productive citizens. We serve other missions by giving them primers and basic Scripture."

4. *Trust God for what is needed.* About finances, Townsend frequently quoted Hudson Taylor: "I don't mind living from hand to mouth, so long as it is God's hand and my mouth."

President Cardenas and U.S. Ambassador to Mexico, Josephus Daniels, became two of Wycliffe's strongest backers. When in Mexico City, Townsend usually called on both men. "Yours is the greatest work in the world," Ambassador Daniels frequently said.

Once during the early days the Townsends were in the capital helping ten new translators obtain travel documents. When President Cardenas heard they had come, he invited them to a banquet in their honor at Chapultepec Castle. His chief of staff picked them up in two limousines and, upon arriving, ushered them into the ornate dining room. The Townsends sat on the president's left and right respectively. Some of the new translators, who had not eaten such a delicious meal since leaving the United States, literally gorged themselves on the nine courses. For such occasions a supply of Spanish New Testaments was carried by Townsend to be given as gifts to officials. Once an official came running after him, saying,

"Hey, Townsend, you forgot to give me one of your little red books."

President Cardenas, who found little good in any religion, once told him, "Of all my friends who come to see me, you are the only one who talks to me about my soul."

While relations between the United States and Mexico were strained over nationalization of foreign oil interests, more new translators were welcomed into the country. In 1940 Herman Aschmann hiked into a Totonac village on a mountainside so steep that corn planters had to tie themselves to boulders to keep from falling out of their fields. Village elders gave him a room back of a saloon; when this proved too noisy, he moved into the jail. Bill Bentley was another of the intrepid pioneers. He hiked into dense jungle near the Guatemalan border and tackled the Mayan Tzeltal dialect. Bentley soon became engaged to translator Marianna Slocum who served an adjoining tribe. When he died of a heart attack at twenty-seven, Marianna and a partner, Florence Gerdel, took over his work with the Tzeltals.

By 1942, fifty Wycliffe Translators were serving over twenty tribes. That year the Ozark training school was moved to the University of Oklahoma and enrolled 130 students.

Townsend began looking toward the numberless tribes in uncharted Amazonia. In 1944 he selected a jungle area in southern Mexico for a survival camp where new recruits could be conditioned for pioneer living. But before the first session opened, his frail wife died.

Two years later he married one of the new Wycliffe girls, Elaine Mielke, who had once been named Chicago's "Outstanding Young Protestant." Former President Cardenas was best man at their wedding and Mrs. Cardenas was matron of honor.

Townsend and his new bride left Mexico to pioneer in Peru. Mexico's ambassador to Peru was then Dr. Moises Saenz, who had helped Townsend enter Mexico. Dr. Saenz helped work out an agreement with the Peruvian government.

With translators to be stationed across a Texas-sized slice of Amazonia, a jungle airline was needed. This was Wycliffe's Jungle Aviation and Radio Service (JAARS). One of the first planes, an $18,000 Catalina, was given by friends in Mexico and named for Dr. Saenz.

Wycliffe translation ministries spread to forty tribes in Peru, leapfrogged into Ecuador (where Rachel Saint and a co-worker translated the first Scriptures for the murderous Aucas), and then spread to Bolivia, Colombia, Brazil, and into Asia and Africa.

Meanwhile back in Mexico, results were showing from long years of patient labor. By 1951 over a thousand Indians had become believers from the Tzeltal tribe which Mexican educators and officials had predicted would "never change." They were matched by a similar number from the neighboring Chol tribe. By the time the Tzeltal and Chol translators finished their New Testaments, over 20,000 were Christians. New believers from Zapotec, Mixtec, Mazatec, Otomi, Tarascan, Huave, Zoque, Totonac, Aztec, and many other tribes shared a new-found faith with the Tzeltals and Chols.

Every Mexican president from Cardenas on has praised Wycliffe's service to the Indians. President Adolfo Mateos (1958-64) served as honorary president of Wycliffe's Mexican Sponsoring Committee and helped the linguists obtain a government lease-gift of five acres of choice land in the capital for a desperately needed new central headquarters building. Mateos and other leading Mexicans joined hands with United States friends to provide funds for the cluster of buildings now valued at over a million dollars and providing space for translators' apartments, offices, printing presses, computers, museum, library, and other necessary functions. In addition, a smaller workshop center for training translation and linguistic consultants for worldwide ministries was built one hundred miles north of Mexico City.

Back in 1965 during my first of eleven trips to Mexico, I sensed the esteem Mexican leaders hold for Wycliffe. I accompanied Cameron Townsend to see Adolfo Lopez Mateos who had just stepped down from the presidency. Without a previous appointment, we were ushered in ahead of a score of waiting dignitaries. After Mateos embraced Townsend in the Latin tradition of good friends, he smiled and said of the pioneer translator, "He is a great am-

bassador. His workers have made great contributions
to our country."

On another visit I flew with Missionary Aviation
Fellowship in the southernmost state of Chiapas.
We skipped over isolated Indian villages, still un-
reached by roads, that now bear the names of such
Bible towns as Nazareth, Bethlehem, Berea. Why
such names? "The influence of Bible translation,"
Pilot E. W. Hatcher said.

Later I met a handsome young Totonac Indian in
Mexico City named Manuel Arenas who holds a master's degree and speaks six languages. He had assisted
the first Bible translator to his people and now, after
obtaining an education abroad, was going back to
start a Bible school for his people. His story is told
in chapter 10.

Another time I visited an Otomi village in the dry
Mesquital Valley. Near a hut made of cactus stalks,
I saw a thirsty child gulping fresh water from a con-
crete basin. The water had been piped in by the
government at the request of the local Wycliffe translator. The miracle which Bible translation has produced among the Otomis is recounted in chapter 2.

On my first trip to Mexico I met Hugh Steven, a tall
blond Canadian member of Wycliffe with a flair for
writing and photography. We decided to jointly prepare this book. Hugh's long residence in Mexico and
his empathy with Indian cultures make him an excel-
lent colleague.

On my most recent trip I talked with Dr. Frank

Robbins, Wycliffe's Mexico director. Dr. Robbins, a Ph.D. graduate of Cornell University, noted that 361 Wycliffe workers were serving 95 Indian tribes and added with a smile, "Lately, I've hardly had time for anything except to attend the dedication of tribal New Testaments. But would you believe there are still a few tribes left to enter?"

I had the last word with Cameron Townsend as he shared the experience of two trips to the USSR at the invitation of the Soviet Academy of Science. "There are 168 languages in Russia," he beamed in anticipation. "Russian linguists are outstanding in their accomplishments. They showed us every courtesy and no opposition to our Bible-translation program. They want us to come back and we plan to do so as soon as arrangements can be worked out."

"Marvelous!" I exclaimed. "How did this miracle happen?"

"It's the Lord's doing," he replied. "It started right here in Mexico City when Mexican friends introduced me to Russian diplomats."

An hour later he was saying, "And when we got to Moscow, the Mexican ambassador received us with open arms. He just couldn't do enough for us."

I knew why.

And, hopefully, you will too after you read these true dramas of *Miracles in Mexico.*

J.C.H

2

Tino: Tribesman, Technician, Teacher

NINETY MINUTES after Neil Armstrong raised the first American flag on the moon's pock-marked surface, President Nixon spoke to the men of Apollo 11. "I am talking to you from the White House," he said. "For every American this has to be the proudest day of our lives. And for people all over the world . . . ."

President Nixon was right. The June 29, 1969, moon landing was a magnificent achievement. But all did not share his personal enthusiasm. Fifteen hundred miles from the White House, in the cold Mexican mountain town of Huautla de Jiménez, thousands of Mazatec Indians were deeply upset and fearful. "It is wrong," they said, "for man to disturb the heavens. The gods of air, wind, and sky will bring sickness and death to us all."

When the Asian flu swept through the 9,000-foot mountain town, seven months later, it left many dead or disabled. The Mazatecs shook their heads and blamed the American astronauts for bringing the disease back from the moon. Then on a cold February afternoon in the middle of the epidemic, a soothing voice came out of their black plastic transistor radios.

"This is the Mazatec Cultural Program," said the voice. Before the startled Mazatecs could ask how it was that the radio man spoke their language, the tinny clash of Mazatec Indian music began to play. First the vibrating strings of a Spanish guitar; then the magic of their own homemade fifty-three-string, thirty-note zither. After a short musical interlude, the man again began to speak. His voice was slow, clear, and easy to understand. From his accent and the way he handled the Mazatec tone and vocabulary, the townspeople knew the speaker was one of them.

"I want to talk to you today," the man said, "about the sickness which stalks our land. All over the world people are sick; across the ocean in England and Asia, and on this side of the ocean in the United States, in Mexico and in South America. It is said by some that the men who reached the moon brought this sickness back with them. This is not at all true. When they arrived back they were immediately locked up in a little house, and doctors tested them to see if they had brought back any sickness. For three weeks they were kept under quarantine. It isn't good that we get frightened by any little thing and that we pass on to each other rumors which are not true. It is better that we take medicine if we get sick.

"Now I will read you a few words from the New Testament in Mazatec. It says: There is nothing that enters into a man which is able to defile him, but what comes out of his heart is what corrupts a man. From within come evil thoughts, adultery, fornication, murder, theft, jealousy, wickedness, deceit, shamelessness, lustful eyes, evil designs, foolishness; all such wickedness comes out of the heart of people. This is what destroys people.

"Just a few words I say to you. These things do us harm. If you want to change and have your heart cleansed, ask the Lord Jesus. He alone can pardon your sins. And of you who have heard, if you have a question to ask about how you can buy a copy of God's Word, write this address: Programa Cultural Mazateco, Apartado Postal 22140, Mexico 22, D.F."

In five short minutes, Fortino "Tino" Cortés, a short, serious, bespectacled Mazatec Indian, had begun a new ministry.

Examining Tino's daily eight to ten-hour job at Wycliffe Bible Translators' Mexico City headquarters, one wonders why he should want further responsibility. Employed as a full-time photographic technician in the publications department, Tino spends vacations and most of his free time acquainting his 60,000 compatriates with his Saviour and Friend.

Bob Chaney, Wycliffe's highly skilled publications manager, says, "Tino is intimately connected with the broad responsibility of publishing Scripture portions, reading materials and New Testaments in over a hundred different languages.

"Furthermore," says Bob with a look of honest concern, "Tino is so skilled and important to the whole publications operation that the department would fall apart if he were ever to leave!"

Bob knows and Tino knows his monetary wages would triple if he took a job with a secular publishing or printing firm. But Tino remains. "I believe," he says with a quiet smile, "that working with Wycliffe as technician is part of my ministry and duty for Christ and the Mazatecs."

Tino also feels the same way about his position as assistant pastor in a local Baptist church in Mexico City. Or his service as chaplain and counselor to thirty or more national employees in Wycliffe's Mexico City headquarters complex.

George Cowan, long-time friend of Tino's, who is general director of Wycliffe Bible Translators and the major force in the Mazatec translation of the New Testament, says, "Tino is always ready to spend his own time and money to help spread the good news of Christ's love among the Mazatec people. When I hold a short-term Bible institute or an evangelistic emphasis, Tino works as my colleague and shares more than equal responsibility for the programs. No matter how busy Tino is with other duties, he always has time for more."

When George prepared a series of fifty-six Bible correspondence courses, it was Tino who corrected and returned the lessons. George started the radio program but Tino has the responsibility for the script and arrangement of the weekly program. When inquiries come, it is Tino who answers and follows

through on the details. Since the radio program began in February, 1970, Tino has answered over one
hundred letters and sent out over a dozen New
Testaments. "In a nonliterate culture, and with poor
mail service," said George, "a hundred letters is a
phenomenal response."

Dr. Benjamin Elson, Wycliffe's executive director
and one-time Mexico branch director, said, "As a
young man, Tino showed strong intelligence and
leadership ability. He had one of the most difficult
of all jobs as a spiritual counselor to our national
employees. Many of the problems he mediated were
difficult and often grave. In each case he showed
great spiritual maturity and depth."

Tino demonstrates the same ability when he con-
ducts a Bible study. "It doesn't matter to me," said one
American missionary, "that Tino has only the equivalent of a sixth-grade education. When he holds a Bible
study, I plan to attend. His spiritual perception and
ability to teach is as good or better than many American Bible teachers I have heard!"

George Cowan remembers Tino as a little orphaned
barefoot Indian boy who used to shout newly memo-
rized Scripture verses at the top of his voice while
hoeing weeds in the steep mountain cornfields.

"When just a boy of ten," said George, "he seemed
to understand that God had a special place of ministry
for him. One day while recording gospel records, he
prayed, 'Help me to speak clearly so those of my

people who are too old to read will hear Your Word and believe in Your Son, Jesus Christ.' "

During most of the years since Tino prayed those words, he has spoken clearly and often. Now through radio, Tino Cortés, an unlettered Mazatec Indian, speaks out clearly and with the same prayer he prayed thirty years before—so that they will hear His Word and believe in His Son, Jesus Christ.

H.S

3

Shepherd of the Desert

A SEARING DESERT WIND tugged at Venancio's tattered straw sombrero. He pulled it tighter over his brown forehead and ran barefoot after a stray lamb that was darting among the giant cacti of the Mesquital desert in Central Mexico.

Driving the stray back to the flock, he continued moving the sheep across the hot sand to the grazing land. When they reached the spot where a few patches of green dotted the brown hill, Venancio perched his brown body on a round rock and took out his dog-eared Spanish primer.

"Yo tengo veinte pesos. Ud. tiene veinte pesos." (I have twenty pesos. You have twenty pesos.)

He jingled the few coins in his pocket. In truth he did not have enough centavos to make even one peso. A Mesquital Otomi Indian shepherd like himself would not earn twenty pesos—less than two American dollars—in a month. Otomi skills were limited to tending sheep, weaving, and scraping a bare living out of corn and beans from the dry soil.

Venancio closed his eyes and dreamed. *If I can learn Spanish and get an education. If . . . .* There were always ifs. He was a teenager and could barely read. His shepherding duties limited his attendance at the village reading class to only one day a week. His Mexican teacher encouraged him, even tutored him some on weekends, and he could study while watching his father's flock. But that was all.

Venancio kept studying and reading any printed matter he could find. At the big market in Ixmiquilpan he handed over his precious centavos for faded pamphlets. For ten centavos he bought instructions on how to read palms. This kindled his thirst more. Soon he and his cousin Tito had an assortment of pamphlets on magic which they could practice on fellow Otomis. *Here,* Venancio thought, *is a way to become a success.*

But magic and sorcery took second place to romance for a while. Isidra's family had built a cactus hut in the village of San Nicolas where Venancio lived. He had seen her spinning and weaving and had decided she would make a good wife to grind the corn for his tortillas.

He built his own little cactus hut on a corner of his father's dry land. Then he checked with both Otomi families to make sure there would be no tribal objection. There wasn't, so the shepherd boy took Isidra into his hut to grind his corn and help tend his flock.

One sultry day Venancio announced to Isidra, "I'm going to be a merchant."

Isidra sighed in relief, "That is better than magic."

Venancio invested his few pesos of savings in a bundle of trinkets sold in Indian markets—knives, ribbons, earrings, safety pins—and began the life of a market merchant.

A chain of colorful Indian markets is held on different days in the Mesquital Valley. The merchants go from one market to another—Zimapán on Sunday, Ixmiquilpan on Monday, Actopan on Wednesday, and so on—offering trinkets, cloth, knives and other goods to Otomis. For such wonders the Otomis trade the fiber products from the century plant of the desert and coarse wool from their sheep. They also sell farm products from the small desert plots which border their cactus homes. Market day is the social event of the week for Otomi families who enjoy the visiting and gossiping as much as the buying and selling.

"I found a new book in the market—a strange book," Tito told Venancio one day. Venancio took the small volume titled *La Santa Biblia* and flipped the pages.

"We will study it together, cousin," Venancio said in their familiar Otomi language. "We will learn things no Otomi has ever known."

The two cousins began studying the strange Book. "It's different from all we have read before," Venancio concluded one day. "What if it is the true Book of God?"

Tito's round eyes swelled. "Then the customs of our people are wrong and foolish."

Venancio nodded soberly. "We must study more."

Months of study convinced them that this was indeed the true Book of God. "This is the way," Venancio said with his finger on a key verse. "I will like the old way no more. I will ask God to take my sins away. I will follow Jesus."

"Sí," Tito agreed. "I will follow Jesus too."

Isidra noted with suspicion their intense interest in the Scriptures. Sometimes the two cousins would sit cross-legged by the driftwood fire on the floor of the hut and talk through the night hours. When others in the village began joining them, she became alarmed.

"You are teaching our neighbors that the customs of our fathers are wrong," she accused her husband one day.

"Sí, but I am teaching them the true way of God."

"We will suffer," she said, wagging a slim finger in his face.

When Venancio tried to teach Isidra from the Book, she became angry. Stuffing her fingers into her ears, she shouted, "Stop! The gods will be angry!"

Venancio turned sadly away. By tribal custom he could have beaten her and forced her to listen. "I will not beat you, or even curse you," he said quietly. "I will ask God to change your heart."

Many statements in the Book were hard for Venancio to understand. Often he wished for someone to help him, but among the 90,000 Otomis who lived in the Mesquital Valley, there was not a single qualified guide. Apparently he and Tito possessed the only Bible in the tribe.

One day in a market he was arranging his trinkets for sale when a Mexican vendor came by. "Buenos días," the Mexican said in a friendly greeting.

Venancio returned the greeting, then courteously asked the stranger's home city.

"Mexico City," the Mexican explained. "I have been a market merchant for many years."

As they talked, the friendly Mexican offered some selling pointers, then quietly introduced a new topic into the conversation by mentioning how much God loves everyone.

Venancio listened eagerly. He asked, "Where did you find out about God's love?"

"In a Book called the Holy Scriptures."

"Is that the same as 'the Holy Bible'?" Venancio asked.

The Mexican nodded. Venancio excitedly told about the Bible he and Tito had been reading. Both Otomi and the Mexican forgot about merchandise as the Mexican explained the basic doctrines of biblical Christianity.

Late in the day, Venancio said, "I will be here next week. Can we talk more?"

"Certainly, brother," the Mexican said. "We will trade and talk about the Scriptures."

So week after week the conversations continued while Venancio grew stronger in the faith. Then his wife became seriously ill.

"Dear Isidra," he whispered, "you need not pray

to the idols. God will help you get well and you will believe as I do."

The crisis finally passed and Isidra began regaining her strength. Venancio noticed that she no longer protested when Tito and others came to talk about the Book.

One evening he came into the hut and heard her sobbing. Isidra lay on the dirt floor prostrate before the Bible. She was asking its forgiveness!

"No, dear Isidra," he said, grasping her hand. "Pray not to the Book, but to the God of the Book."

She did. From that day she was a changed person and Venancio's strongest supporter as they studied the Bible together.

Many of Venancio's neighbors came to believe as the witness spread from hut to hut. Then in 1933 a stranger arrived in the Mesquital Valley. The tall American introduced himself as Richmond McKinney. "I have come to put the Bible into your own language," he said.

Venancio felt like dancing for joy. "God's Book in Otomi!" Then a thought chilled his heart. "No one has written down our language. There is not a book in Otomi in the world."

It was true. The poor Otomis had been living in the desert valley for centuries, how long, no one really knew for certain, and their language had remained locked in the tribe. Only about half of them knew enough market Spanish to talk with the Mexican traders.

McKinney had come to Mexico with W. Cameron Townsend and eight other translators. He had been one of the first two students in the linguistic school established at Sulphur Springs, Arkansas, by Townsend and L. L. Legters in 1931.

Venancio and his fellow believers eagerly offered to help. McKinney became the first missionary to learn Otomi, and soon Otomi believers knew a few Bible verses in their own language.

Then the winds of ridicule and criticism swooped down upon the Otomi Christians.

"They study a book written by lying spirits."

"They deny the customs of our tribe."

"They do not take food to the graves of our dead."

"They do not hang a skull in their gardens to frighten away the evil spirits."

"They do not give their quota for the pulque (century-plant beer) for the fiesta."

Venancio noticed that their old friends no longer walked with them to market, but only passed by and glared silently at them. Venancio's business dropped off. Then the village leaders of San Nicolas asked Venancio and Isidra to leave. "If you stay," they warned, "we cannot guarantee your safety."

The couple found a bare hill overlooking the market-center town of Ixmiquilpan and obtained permission to build a cactus hut there. Tito and his wife joined them and, as time passed, more cactus huts were built on the hill by believers driven from their old homes at gunpoint. The believers built a church and asked Venancio to be their spiritual shepherd.

One afternoon when Pastor Venancio was away, the believers noticed the people in the big town below talking together in clusters. "We're afraid, Isidra," they told her. "They are plotting evil."

Isidra, now strong in the faith, chided the fearful. "Is God dead? No! Let's get the people to pray!"

She hurried barefoot from hut to hut, asking the people to pray. She felt something was planned for that night, perhaps a mob attack. She prayed with the believers and they went to bed and slept peacefully.

Next day in the town they saw people talking in groups and pointing to them. From a few fanatics willing to talk, they pieced together this story!

On the night before, several hundred enemies of the Christians had gathered back of the hill, armed with dynamite, guns, and machetes. On a signal they started up the hill. Suddenly the forward marchers halted. The little church stood outlined in a glaring light that shone over the hilltop. Soldiers encircled the hilltop, holding guns in firing position. They heard trumpets. Suddenly they turned and ran in terror.

A miracle? The Otomi believers think to this day that God intervened in their behalf.

But the fanatical opponents of the gospel planned another attack.

A collection was started to hire killers to wipe out

the Christians. Old Mary, notoriously wicked, wanted
to be the first to contribute. She gave two hundred
pesos, proceeds from her sales of pulque beer. Hating
the believers because they did not drink, she had
daily cursed them as they passed by where she was
selling pulque.

Many attempts were made on believers' lives. Only
one was successful. A nineteen-year-old Christian
was beaten to death. And still the colony on the hill
grew. Old Mary wondered.

The Christians continued to pray for her, and slowly,
strangely, Old Mary's heart melted. One day she, too,
accepted Christ.

She stopped selling the pulque drink. Then persecution came to her village early one Sunday morning.
Fanatics beat the believers with sticks, stones and
machetes. Old Mary received ten big bruises. Sore
and aching, Old Mary and her fellow believers walked
to the Christian colony on the hill for worship. She
told the story of the beatings to Pastor Venancio.

When she finished, he smiled. "Sister Mary, didn't
you pay two hundred *pesos* last year to have the
brethren killed?" She nodded. "Well, you paid in
advance twenty pesos for each of your bruises." Those
standing around laughed. Then they went into church
to worship the God whom they loved more than life.

The translation work marched along with the growth
of the believers. McKinney, the first translator, was
replaced by a couple, Don and Isabel Sinclair. Ethel
Wallis, a graduate of the University of California

at Los Angeles, came in 1941. Other single-girl translators followed her.

The government of Mexico began pushing a literacy
campaign among the Mesquital Otomis and with the
help of Wycliffe Translators published school material
in the Otomi language. Eighty Otomi schoolteachers
were trained by Wycliffe workers to teach Otomi
children to read first in their mother tongue, and then
in Spanish.

As literacy grew among the Otomis, the translators
pushed ahead, knowing that a large body of potential
Bible readers was arising. A translation center to
serve missionaries from all over Mexico was con-
structed a short distance from the Christian village
on the hill.

"Otomis are a pastoral and agricultural people,"
Ethel Wallis notes. "Many biblical symbols are familiar
to them. When we came to Saul's 'kicking against the
pricks,' they knew immediately what this meant.
Otomi farmers plow with oxen and when an animal
balks or resists, he pushes his flesh against a sharp
goad. They understand the symbolism of the good
Shepherd and the lost sheep. A few sheep are the only
'wealth' of many families. They grasped the signifi-
cance of Jesus' declaration, 'I am the water of life,'
for their meager crops and life itself depend upon the
infrequent rains."

Ethel recalls one drought that lasted five years:
"There were a few showers, but not enough to prepare
the ground for crops. The water holes shriveled up to

scum and dregs. Both animals and people were dying. The saddest were the little children who could draw no milk from their mothers' breasts. Many died of malnutrition and of exposure to cold winter temperatures."

Ethel persuaded government officials to send a tank truck filled with water into Otomi country. This was the start of a water-hauling program that lasted for eighteen months until a deep well was dug and pipes laid to transport water to the village where Ethel Wallis and two other translators now live. The government also established a health center nearby for the Otomis.

In recent years persecution of the believers has lessened in the valley. Fanatics, steeped in paganism and a perverted form of Catholicism, have learned that the Mexican government insists on complete religious freedom. There are now about three thousand believers in some thirty congregations scattered throughout the dry valley. The Otomi New Testament was published last year.

Pastor Venancio serves the believers on the hill above Ixmiquilpan and evangelizes in outlying villages. Other native pastors serve local congregations in distant villages, many of which meet in cactus chapels.

The Mesquital believers have sent out their own "foreign missionaries" to the Huichol tribe in northern Mexico. They have encouraged the few Huichol believers who have suffered persecution from their own tribespeople.

"The pioneer saints of the Mesquital Otomis have encouraged us who serve as translators among them," Ethel Wallis says. "They are so terribly poor, yet so bold in their witness and so rich in the kingdom of love.

"Many of the Otomis," Ethel declares, "have died from disease and lack of proper nourishment. Easter is a great day for them. It's truly resurrection Sunday."

Pastor Venancio's darkest trial came when his beloved Isidra died. Christian Otomi women dressed her in a cheap white satin shroud and placed her in a humble casket. Her funeral was held on Easter Sunday. All day the believers sang hymns about resurrection and heaven around the casket. They sang, "I am a pilgrim, I'm going to heaven to live with Jesus eternally," "There is no sadness in heaven," and many other hymns. Between songs, Venancio and other brethren read Scripture, prayed, cried, and even rejoiced.

When the sun sank behind the big hill where the believers lived, Venancio was still standing at the head of the grave. He was holding his little Conchita, who was too young to weep, and wiping his own tears away with a big red handkerchief. As the last stone was put down, someone prayed, "God, comfort our brokenhearted brother and his motherless children."

The Otomi Christian village on the hill above Ixmiquilpan is today a showplace in the area. Cactus huts have been replaced by sturdy stone and adobe ones. Pastor Venancio's people practice sharing and helpfulness similar to what the first-century church at Jerusalem did. They have purchased a farm and developed new ways of farming, weaving, and making rope. They have installed a good drainage and sewer system for the village.

Literacy and manual skills are taught to any person who wishes to learn. Young people are encouraged to study beyond the local schools. Some are being trained as nurses.

Recently a government official, involved in the economic upgrading of the poverty-stricken Otomis, was asked what the government had done for Pastor Venancio's village.

He replied: "Nothing. They don't need help. We hire them to show others how to help themselves."

J.C.H.

4

An Aztec Merchant Meets the Master

RAIN DOESN'T FALL in the south central state of
Puebla, Mexico—it is thrown. Ten feet of it per year.
Mules and men slip, slide, and sink to their knees
in oozy red mud. Sunlight seldom penetrates the
overhanging trees along the main trade route leading
from the Sierra Aztec village of Tatoscac to the
Gulf of Mexico.

Twenty years of driving mules through mud,
shivering cold, fog, and pelting rain reduces a man
to a notch below the obstinate beasts he drives.

Sevriano Mancilla Lopez was such a man: short,
barrel-chested, with bushy black hair on a head too
big for his shoulders. His face shone like polished
bronze when he shaved—which was almost never.

Only his mules understood the extraordinary mixture of Spanish and Aztec profanities which he used
liberally on both mules and man.

Once each week Sevriano loaded his mules with
coffee, pottery, and vegetables, said good-bye to his
wife Carmen and family in Tatoscac, then pushed his

51

mules thirty miles to the coast. There he quickly un-
loaded his merchandise, said hello, and settled in with
his wife Chala and family number two. This routine
he broke only for fiestas.

To an American, fiesta connotes gaiety, laughter,
and happy abandon. To mountain Aztec tribepeople
in Mexico, it means three to four days of around-the-
clock, ear-shattering brassy band "music" and sense-
less drinking. Drinking as lustily as he swore, Sevriano
usually ended each fiesta rolling in the dirt, too
drunk from pulque beer to find his way home.

Sevriano's profession as a traveling merchant dates
back over five hundred years. Hernan Cortez, conqueror of Mexico, discovered Aztec trade routes
extending south from Mexico City to Yucatán and
Guatemala. Dressed in impeccable cotton tunics, the
trade merchants, or *Pochteca* as they were called,
purchased tons of corn, beans, cotton, rubber balls,
brilliant bales of feathers, obsidian, and jade. These
were paid each year as tribute to Aztec king, Monte-
zuma.

The traveling merchant was the trailblazer of the
Aztec empire. Often acting as a spy, he reported to
the king all activities in his province. Because the
merchant was appointed by royal decree, he had
the quality and dignity of an ambassador. Mistreatment
or injury to a merchant was considered an affront to
royal dignity.

The morning Sevriano met Bible translator Dow
Robinson, he hardly bore the image of his noble

Aztec forebears. Mud splotched his black stubbly beard. The coarse wool poncho draped over his shoulder was thick with a mixture of mule and man odor. His once-white palm sombrero perched on his massive head like a glob of ice cream ready to slip off the cone.

"Ho, you black snake of the mountain!" At Sevriano's command, the big lead mule stumbled to a stop along the trail side, curled his tongue around a clump of moist grass, and unceremoniously chomped a midmorning snack.

"Muy buenos días, Don Francisco," he called. (Unable to pronounce "Robinson," Aztecs gave Dow the closest Spanish equivalent.)

"And a good morning to you," replied the boyish-looking American.

Sevriano had heard through the local grapevine that the newly arrived Wycliffe Bible translators, Dow and Lois Robinson, lived in the white house on the main trade route to the coast.

"I stop only to say hello and bid you welcome to our village," the mule driver said in a low, gravelly voice.

After talk of where do you live, do you like living in Tatoscac, and isn't it a nice day, Sevriano leaned over his saddle. He looked right, then left, and in a stage whisper asked Dow if it wasn't true he was learning to speak Aztec so he could sell the language to the government and make money.

Dow looked up into Sevriano's serious black eyes.

"Sevriano," said Dow, "I live in your village and learn your language so every Aztec in Tatoscac and all the Sierras will have God's Word in a book."

"You mean," said Sevriano with astonishment, "the same Scriptures that Evangelicals use in Spanish can be put into Aztec?"

"Yes," said Dow, "the same!"

"I would like to talk more about these things when I return," said Sevriano. With that the mule driver jerked the hemp neck-reins on his riding mule and called out a word prefaced by "lazy," and the five munching mules resumed clomping their way along the muddy trail to the coast.

On future trips Sevriano made it a regular practice to stop and sip a cup of unblended mountain coffee while the Robinsons shared newly translated portions of Scripture with him.

From their first meeting, Sevriano liked Dow. He was unlike the American tourists he occasionally met on the coast. They were tall, light-skinned, and talked in loud voices. Dow was neither tall nor loud, and his skin was the color of light walnut. But it was Dow's honest interest in Sevriano as a person that kept him returning to share coffee and listen to the explanation of the Scriptures.

The people of Tatoscac soon realized that Sevriano was taking more than a passing interest in the translators and their work. Rumors began spreading that he was even attending church services of the *evangelicas.*

"I am beginning to think the Scripture verses we talk about are dangerous," Sevriano said one day.

"Why do you say that?" asked Dow.

"Because," answered Sevriano, "the priest in our village threatens to have me killed!"

"Have you killed!" exclaimed Dow.

"Yes. You see, I argue very much with him and always I tell him what the Bible says. When I repeat Scripture verses to him, he never knows what to say. Last week in the village square he told me he was going to have me killed if I did not stop reading the Scriptures and listening to your lies. I only laughed, but inside I was angry. I asked how can you, a man of God, say you will have me killed when the Scriptures say no one should kill? Oh, Don Francisco, it was funny to see a brown man with a red face."

Primitive communities demand strict conformity to established rules and tradition. Change is seldom tolerated. For example, to put a tin roof on a house in a community of grass roofs invites social separation. Some societies demand physical retribution and destruction of such a house.

Thus it is a serious offense for a tribal member to depart from established religious traditions and practices. More than one Evangelical who refused to drink at fiesta time in honor to Tatoscac's image was shot and left for the buzzards on a back mountain trail.

Aztecs believe any change in tribal tradition brings too much rain, crop failure, sickness and displeasure of tribal gods. To secure the safety and prosperity of the whole tribe, offenders are persuaded to return to the status quo or are eliminated.

For Sevriano to begin a character change was more dramatic than most. Everyone knew he drank like a fish. Usually men who had a second wife tried to keep it a secret. Not Sevriano. He bragged about having a wife at each end of the trail. He was, in fact, a hero in the eyes of lesser men.

It was difficult to tell when the change came. At first Sevriano wasn't willing to admit to any change. Besides, he knew the consequences waiting for people whose thoughts were different. But Nicolas, Tatoscac's leather-faced blacksmith, knew something had changed.

In the past when Sevriano brought a mule to Nicolas for new shoes, the air filled quickly with strong oaths. This was especially true when the mule became excited or uncooperative. This time, to Nicolas' surprise, Sevriano spoke only calm, reassuring words. Not once did he taint the air with an acid word.

"Yes! Yes! It is true. Sevriano is not the man he once was," agreed Alejandro, the village's talkative harness maker, when Nicolas told him the story. "Did you not see him today? What man in the village would not drink until he slept when his only son has died!"

Life and death exist on equal terms in the Aztec Sierras. Sevriano knew death as he knew life. But the pain he felt for the loss of his son was a sting sharper and more painful than any previous sorrow.

For almost two hours he sat with his chin cupped in

his thick bronzed hands. His gaze never lifted from an invisible object on Dow's rough floor.

"I am a man who has over fifty years," he finally said. "Many sadnesses have come to my life. Always before I became drunk to stop the pain in my stomach. Now when the greatest of all sadness comes, I have a different mind and no desire to drink. Before I read the Scripture verses and listened to you and the other brethren, I had no spiritual comfort. It has taken me many years to understand God's message. I want now to begin a new life serving God."

From the beginning, Sevriano took his commitment seriously. "If I am to become a person who speaks truth from God's Book," he told Dow, "I must begin myself to obey completely the words of Scripture."

The words which spoke of keeping one day each week for the Lord disturbed him. "I drive my mules each week over Sunday to the coast. I cannot honor God if I do not come to His house." he told a friend.

Dow never knew exactly when Sevriano sold his mule train. But suddenly he realized, after returning to the village following a long absence, that Sevriano no longer stopped by his house.

"Have you not heard?" said an Indian believer when Dow asked about Sevriano. "He sold his mules and at a great loss."

The merchants on the coast had wanted to pay their debts to him in tobacco and liquor. But he would not accept that kind of payment, so he canceled all that was owed him. This amounted to over five hundred pesos—five years' wages.

"And that's not all." The Indian lowered his voice slightly and continued, "Because the Scriptures speak of having only one wife, he took his children from Chala on the coast and made one family here in Tatoscac."

"And what happened to Chala?" asked Dow. "Did he abandon her?"

"No, no," came the reply. "He sent her back to her father. Now she has become married again."

"Why has Sevriano done this?" questioned Dow.

The Indian looked puzzled that Dow should ask such an obvious question. "Because," came the simple reply, "Sevriano obeys what he reads in Scripture."

Sevriano knew that persecution had to come. At first it came as social pressure. Relatives no longer considered him a member of the family. His mule-driving "friends" tried to entice him with hot words about losing his manhood and pleaded with him to spend a night drinking with them. When he didn't give in, they too ignored him. Each resistance he met with love and, when possible, with a simple explanation of how he was finding spiritual satisfaction and happiness.

When it became evident that Sevriano meant to continue in the new way, an active wave of persecution started against the Evangelicals. Sevriano's house was set to flames and two lay preachers were shot on the trail.

Instead of becoming frightened, the ex-mule driver became immediately concerned over congregations whose pastors no longer held services.

One of these was a small Aztec church set on the pinnacle of a 3,000-foot mountain trail. When Sevriano heard that the preacher could no longer assume his pastoral duties, he stepped in. For three years, without wages or thought of personal safety or comfort, Sevriano walked the tortuous mountain trail each Sunday to witness and encourage the small church.

Even though Sevriano was untrained and his first sermons were crude, the church had the strongest vital faith of any Dow visited.

"He just plugged away for three years and kept the church from falling apart," said Dow. "I visited the church twice and never saw a man so burdened for his congregation. He told me one day that if he didn't preach, the devil would take the whole congregation away!"

After the frontal attack of persecution subsided, Sevriano opened a small general store. It soon became apparent that here was an honest man who could be trusted. He consistently gave correct measure for corn and beans, never overcharged as many merchants did, and treated his clients in a way so dramatically different from his former self that many people actually came to know Christ.

His reputation for honesty elected him to civic responsibility. During his term in office he strengthened the evangelical cause by a nonpartial program of

animal and fruit husbandry. He encouraged the local
school officials to extend the school term from three
to six years.

When Dow returned to the tribe after an absence of
three years in the States where he received his Ph.D.,
he asked Sevriano to help on the translation team.
"Your people understand just enough Spanish to buy
and sell in the market," said Dow. "Some understand
enough Spanish to accept the gospel, but they are
immediately stillborn. To have a strong Aztec church,
the Scriptures in Aztec must be made available to
every believer and congregation in their own tongue."

Dow tutored Sevriano in Bible-translation methods
and principles. At first it was difficult for Sevriano
to learn the discipline of carefully examining words,
sentences, verses and paragraphs for exact meaning
and the thrust of Scripture passages.

While working on Ephesians, Sevriano came to
understand in a new and deeper way that God gave
new life on the inside, not just change on the outside.

"Oh, so that is the meaning!" became a frequent
expression when Dow explained a verse.

At age fifty-five, change is difficult for any man;
but just as soon as Sevriano understood what was
needed, he willingly learned all Dow taught him. "It
showed me again," said Dow, "the fantastic mind and
personality of a man whom many people would con-
sider unfit to teach."

With a clear understanding of the Word in his own
language, Sevriano has become a powerful exhorter.

Standing each Sunday in the center of a congregation of over four-hundred Aztecs and mestizos, Sevriano translates the sermon given by the Spanish-speaking preacher.

"When I first saw him in 1957," exults Dow, "I thought that this was the last man God would ever use for a preacher. He was crude and harsh as any mule driver could be. Hardly what one could call loving. He represents the biggest change in personality structure I have seen anywhere. Today he is considerate, kind, thoughtful, and willing to give himself for other people."

Most of Sevriano's growth has come through his understanding of what the Scriptures say in Aztec. "He is," said Dow, "a Christian gentleman absolutely!"

H.S.

5

The Chamula's Unknown God

DOMINGO HERNANDEZ climbed the steep trail leading
to the mountaintop without looking back to the
scraggly village of thatched huts in the valley from
which he had come. He slashed an occasional vine
that barred his path and kept his eyes on the morning
sun that was beginning to tiptoe over the mountain
in the rugged southern state of Chiapas.

"Domingo, you must hurry and beg the sun-god's
help," his wife had pleaded while he held their in-
jured son. "Next time you might kill one of us."

The Chamula Indian knew his son would recover.
He had only hit him with the blunt edge of his machete.
But the next time the holy drink made him crazy,
he might strike a deathblow to one of his children.

The thought chilled the Indian's stomach in the
cool morning air. There could not be a next time.
The sun-god had to help him overcome his thirst for
the holy drink, a crude corn liquor which the Chamulas
made and offered to the gods.

Now Domingo stood on the mountaintop, arms raised in supplication. He started to pray as his ancestors had done for centuries. "O great god of the sun, send your rays into my poor head. Drive out the evil spirits that make me take the holy drink."

Domingo paused and reflected. He had prayed to the sun-god before and received no help. 'There must be a God greater than the sun-god," he reasoned. "I will pray to Him, though I know not His name."

The Chamula, who had never seen a Bible, began praying to this God whom he did not know. "Help me not to drink," he begged.

After that Domingo amazed his wife and friends by refusing all offers to drink. Then one day his horse wandered away.

"Go to a talking god and ask where the horse has gone," his wife said. "It has always been the custom."

There were numerous talking gods in Chamula territory. Domingo took a chicken and a few pesos and hurried to a hut where one lived. He handed an offering to the god's owner and made his request. Then he sat on the floor, his eyes slanting downward, and waited for the god to speak.

A high-pitched voice came from where the stone idol stood, telling Domingo to go to a certain valley where he would find his horse.

Domingo thanked the god's owner and started home. On the way he stopped to consult another talking god. To his amazement, this god gave him contradictory directions.

One more time he stopped and paid money to the owner of a talking god. This time, as the god was speaking, Domingo leaped to his feet and ran away. When he arrived home, he told his wife, "Our gods have no power. They are ignorant. I will ask the God above all gods to show me where to find my horse."

His wife's eyes widened. "No! Domingo, no! The elders will kill you for speaking this way."

But Domingo was already praying, asking for guidance from the God he did not yet know.

The next morning he leaped from the mat where he had been sleeping. "I saw my horse in a dream last night!" he shouted. "I saw where it is grazing." Then he ran out of the hut and after a long trip reached the place. There stood his mare with a newborn colt.

When he arrived home with the mare and colt, he declared, "Never again will I pray to the gods of our people. They are of no help."

His wife began wringing her hands. "No Chamula has ever talked this way and lived. Please, Domingo, please be silent!"

"Be silent!" Domingo exclaimed. "What have the Chamula gods brought us? The cursed holy drink that makes me beat my son. Debt for us and riches to the owners of the gods. Power to the elders who rule over us. Pack me some food," he commanded. "I am going to the market town to find work."

* * *

In the market town of Las Casas, Wycliffe translators Ken and Elaine Jacobs were praying. "Lord,

William Cameron Townsend, left, founder of Wycliffe Bible Translators, with old friends, Dr. and Mrs. George Cross, at Wycliffe's new Mexico City headquarters. For 25 years Dr. Cross was president of the University of Oklahoma, site of Wycliffe's linguistic training courses.

Gamio Translation Center in central Mexico, where translators and language assistants come for concentrated study.

Tino Cortes, top, Mazatec photographic technician in Wycliffe's Mexico City office, heads up a radio program, "Programa Cultural Mazeteco." A dialogue radio message is given by Antonio and Tino, while below Constantino and Aurelio record native Mazatec music on native instruments.

Translator Katherine Voigtlander stands with an eastern Otomi family in front of a mosaic she designed for Mexico City headquarters. Below, Sevriano, an Aztec merchant, pushed 30 miles to market at the coast every week before he found Christ.

The oldest Chamula Indian, "Grandma," was among the group driven out of translator Ken Jacob's house by Chamula elders expelling believers from the tribe. The middle picture shows Domingo, a Chamula Christian leader, and his daughter, Maruch. Below, David Jarvis, Wycliffe missionary, and Juan Mucha, Tzeltal Christian, discuss revolutionary agricultural approach-terracing.

Esther Burgess, left, is a second generation Wycliffe translator to work among the Tarahumara Indians. Below, Nick ("Tell Us Where God Lives") and his wife show off their garden—the first in the village, while below Nick handles medical duties.

Andy, right, was the first Chinantec to "grab hold of the Word of God." Below, Cal Rensch shares translated Scriptures, a Chinantec holds a hymn book, and the Tomato Gulch jail that held seven believers for three days.

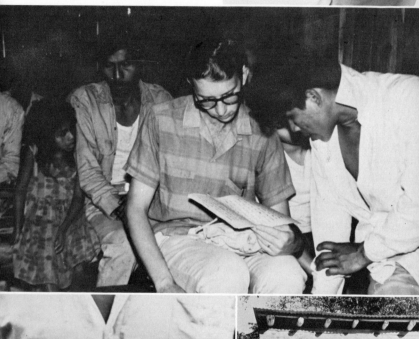

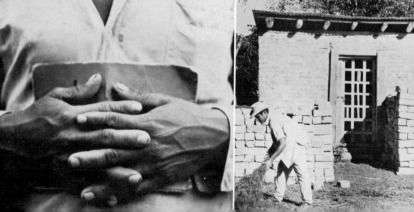

Totonac women like these learned to read the Word of God when
sold a copy on their first visit to the city.

Manual Arenas, right, is a brilliant Totonac Indian who is a product of Bible translation. Below, a re-enaction of an ancient Aztec ceremony and a pyramid temple of the Mayan period. Bottom, a Missionary Aviation Fellowshhip plane has brought Viola Warkentin to the Cholos, who are Mayan descendents.

we want to give the Chamulas Thy Word," Ken said. "But how can we without a language helper? We trust You to send us one, for the elders will not permit us to live in the tribe."

Two years before, the Jacobs had moved to the town of Las Casas near Chamula territory in the southern Mexican state of Chiapas. Numbering about 45,000 and living in a mountainous 1,000-square-mile area, the Chamulas had forcibly resisted all advances from outsiders. A hundred years earlier, they had driven out the Mexican priests who had tried to win them to Roman Catholicism. After expelling the outsiders, the Chamula elders did something which horrified government officials. They impaled a witch doctor's young son on a cross and proclaimed the boy to be their savior.

An old man had helped Ken and Elaine learn a few Chamula words. But he had died without ever showing any sign of interest in the gospel. Now they needed a younger man who could not only help them with the language, but become the first Chamula believer.

One afternoon Domingo Hernandez came to the Jacobs' door. He spoke in crude Spanish and asked for work. When Ken replied in Chamula, Domingo beamed. "I will pay you to care for our garden," Ken said, "if you will teach me your tongue."

Domingo nodded his agreement. Soon Ken and Domingo were translating the gospel of Mark into Chamula. Ken eagerly watched Domingo's rising interest, but two years passed without the Chamula ever saying he believed in the true God.

One evening they were standing before the fireplace and talking about the day's work. There came a period of silence, then Domingo said softly, "My people don't know yet."

After the Chamula had gone to bed, Ken said to Elaine, "What is it that Domingo's people don't know? Is Domingo a secret believer? I wonder."

A few days later Domingo left on one of his periodic visits to his family in the tribe. Upon returning, he invited Ken and Elaine to dedicate his new house. "When a Chamula builds a new house," he explained, "he makes sacrifices to the evil spirits so they will not eat the souls of his children. I want to dedicate my house to the true God and His Son, Jesus. Please come and help me."

Ken and Elaine were aware of the danger, but they went. They joined about forty-five people squeezed into the one-room, thatch-roofed hut. Domingo and the men sat on one side and the women sat on the floor.

Ken listened in wonder as Domingo thanked God for the new house. Then Domingo asked Ken to lead in some hymns. When Domingo prayed again, he broke into sobs while praying that his relatives and neighbors might know about Christ.

The translators left about midnight to make the long trip back to Las Casas. They feared to stay in Chamula territory overnight.

After they left, a witch doctor warned Domingo, "Give up your evil beliefs or your children will die."

Domingo slowly shook his head. "They will not die. God will protect them."

A few weeks later Domingo told Ken, "There are now nine families who trust in Jesus, and we are meeting together for worship and Bible study. But already my enemies have tried to kill me and burn my house down. We will not stop," he vowed. "We will go on following Jesus."

The persecution became worse and one afternoon a truck stopped in front of the Jacobs' home in Las Casas. Domingo led forty Chamula men, women, and children into the yard. "The elders have chased us from our homes," he told Ken sadly. "We have nowhere to go and nothing to eat."

Ken and Elaine shared their food and every available sleeping space in their one-bedroom house. One Chamula family slept in the corn bin; another in the wheat bin. Two families stayed in the tiny one-room hut where Domingo had slept while working for the translators.

Ken and Domingo went to the Mexican Director of Indian Affairs and asked for help and advice. "I will help you and your friends find work," the official told Domingo. "But you must not try to go back until I talk with the elders. They are denying you religious freedom."

The official went into the tribe and conferred with the elders. "What have they done?" he asked. "They

have not killed, stolen, or kidnapped women. They
only wish to worship in their own way."

"But this is contrary to the laws of our fathers,"
the elders said. "We cannot allow it."

"You will allow it," the official said sternly, "or
the government will send in soldiers."

Finally the elders consented for the Christians to
return, except for Domingo and one other leader who
could be in the tribe only during the day. "We cannot
be responsible for their safety at night," the elders
said.

One evening a band of Chamula men surrounded
the house of a Christian family. Without a word of
warning, they unslung their machetes and cocked
their shotguns. One squirted gasoline on the thick
thatched roof.

Inside, five people slept unaware of danger: four
young sisters and an eighteen-year-old baby-sitter
named Pacu.

The acid fumes from the burning roof awoke Pacu.
She screamed frantically for the children to flee.
When Pacu's head appeared in the doorway, one of
the marauders fired point-blank into her face.

Momentarily she slumped; then, gathering every
ounce of strength, she ran into the cornfield. Some-
how she found the house of her uncle and was saved.

The four sisters were not so fortunate. In the morning light, authorities found the charred remains of
one young girl in the ashes. The others were nearby
in a cooplike structure, all seriously wounded. Only

two reached the hospital in Las Casas. One died on the way.

Mexican authorities have clamped down harder on the Chamula elders who have tried to resist the gospel with force. Domingo and the Chamula Christians who look to him for leadership are standing firm. They are trusting in the true God who has become a vital reality in their lives.

J.C.H.

6

Is It a True Word
That God Speaks in a Book?

ONE DARK NIGHT twenty years ago, Tzeltal Indian
Juan Mucha carried a pitch-pine torch and walked
over a rock mountain trail in southwest Mexico to
the house of newly arrived Wycliffe Bible translators
Marianna Slocum and Florence Gerdel. When Marianna opened the door to his knock, Juan shyly asked
an outstanding question.

"I have heard," he said quietly, "that God speaks
in a book. Is that a true word?"

Marianna, surprised with his forthright question,
said, "Yes. Yes! It is a true word. Come inside and
we will tell you why we have come to your mountain."

Juan extinguished his torch and stepped inside the
small split-cedar shake house. Marianna, in a soft
cultured Philadelphia accent, told Juan that it was
her plan to translate into his own Tzeltal language
the very words God had spoken.

After listening to Marianna's explanation, Juan

reached into his woven-palm carrying bag and pulled out a small notebook and pencil. With large brown innocent eyes, he looked up into Marianna's face and said, "If what you say is a true word, then I have come to write down all God has said."

The unusual encounter with Juan resulted in Marianna and Florence moving to his village of Corralito. Almost immediately Juan provided the strong quiet leadership so important to a fledgling work. His ability to live out a vigorous practical Christianity became legendary among the Tzeltal Christians.

The most notable example has been Juan's struggle against slash-and-burn agriculture. For centuries the Tzeltals have practiced this destructive form of farming, leaving a blasted, weak, eroded land unsuitable for sustained farming.

The Tzeltals responded to the good news of spiritual cleanliness through Marianna's translated Scriptures. They also accepted Florence's practical application of modern medicine. But ironically, the translators' work became the source of another problem. Disease had kept the battle for life on death's side. Now, because of antibiotics and the application of personal hygiene, fewer Tzeltals died. The increased population meant a greater demand for food. The small valley of less than five-hundred acres was unable to produce enough food for 22,000 Highland Tzeltals.

Juan knew as keenly as anyone the struggle to keep his large family in corn from planting to harvest.

His first wife died after childbirth because for too long she had given food to her children that she needed herself.

Juan's gospel of land improvements was inaugurated when David Jarvis, a lank English agronomist, joined Wycliffe's ranks to assist in the Tzeltal work. One day Juan and David stood on a hill looking out over the small valley.

"Juan," said David in his broad accent, "we need to convince your people that terracing the mountainsides and using barnyard manure will help solve the food-shortage problem."

"Yes," said Juan, "we Tzeltals are hard to change." Then he added thoughtfully, "Why not begin on my land?"

During the church service the following Sunday, Juan Mucha, in as serious a look as his impish face would allow, told the surprised congregation that beginning Monday morning "Grandfather" David would pay money for manure. There was a long moment of silence and then gales of laughter. But several days later a small girl appeared at Jarvis' door.

"Grandfather David," she said hesitantly, "is it a true word that you buy these things? It's not a false word?"

David said, "No, it is a true word." With that, the girl raced back down the trail where she had left a small bundle of manure wrapped in a banana leaf. This shy beginning started a great train of men hauling manure to Jarvis' backyard.

Using a pickax and guidance from David, Juan cleared and terraced over half an acre of hillside.

"We see you do the work of children," taunted the skeptics as they saw Juan make the strange ridges around the hill.

Smiling broadly, Juan would try to explain that by doing this he would get a bigger crop on less land space. When the skeptics heard this, they cut his words to ribbons with snickers and laughter. They would walk slowly away, wagging their heads, saying Juan must have the brain of a burro.

Pain, loss of possessions, and death are things that the Tzeltal accepts with bravery and stoicism. But ridicule and criticism are like a hot knife to his heart. Juan faced his months of ridicule and uncertainty with uncommon grace and patience. He firmly believed his first crop would convince the skeptics. But his first crop failed!

Bravely, Juan tried a second time, but only a small fraction of his crop produced. When Juan tried the third year, villagers knew he was crazy and spent most of their time telling him so.

"Lord," prayed Juan after he planted the third time, "if You can make some of the plants grow, You can make them all grow."

And grow they did! That year Juan stopped the criticism of his neighbors by producing ten times more beans than anyone else. The slash-and-burn methods produced five pods per bean plant. Juan's produced fifty. Corn on the old ground gave a small fifteen-centimeter ear. Juan's was twenty-seven centimeters long and weighed nearly a pound.

It has taken nearly nine years, but now most of the Tzeltal Christians are convinced that, even though it looks like child's work, terracing pays off. Juan is especially convincing as he uses Scripture to reinforce the gospel of land improvement: 2 Corinthians 5:17 is Juan's most powerful weapon. "If any one is in Christ . . . The new has come" (Berkeley).

"What does this mean?" Juan asks each Tzeltal family he visits. "Does this mean just our souls? Doesn't it mean the way we treat our wives and how we teach our children? Doesn't it mean the condition of our homes, our land?"

Nearly always when Tzeltal men hear this explanation they become ashamed of their lack of response to practical Christian living. Juan then leaves and lets them think about what he said. In a few days he returns and voluntarily helps the family begin their own terracing.

Juan doesn't fit the traditional mold of a backward Indian. He is continually thinking up new ideas. Recently he built a fish tank and dug a canal from the river to his home. Since the canal is below his house, he plans to put a little water wheel on the drop-out side so he can have electricity. He has made canoes, wheelbarrows, and a large platform for a two-story house. Using old cans, he made a telephone that goes 150 feet to the house of his cousin. And it works!

But best of all, Juan is the pacesetter for the Tzeltal

Christians in Corralito. He has never forgotten that his central task is to live out all God has spoken.

H.S.

7

Tarahumara Triumph

THE SIERRA MADRE WIND whistled eerily through the thick Ponderosa pines that swayed over the Tarahumara settlement of Samachique. The mountain village lay quiet in respect for the tribal elders who were questioning a chief's son.

The prosecutor pulled his blanket about him to shut out the chill and spoke gruffly to the slim boy who faced the elders. "You, Ramon, do you deny helping the 'outsiders'?"

"Honored sir, the 'outsiders' are writing down our words. I have helped them, yes. How else would they learn?"

The questioner pitched his voice to a sarcastic whine. "And you have also taken their religion and customs to be your own? The beliefs of our ancestors are not good enough for you?"

Ramon's dark eyes flashed. "I believe in Jesus. He is the Son of the true God. But I remain a Tarahumara."

"You are still a Tarahumara? You do not listen to our medicine men. You take the outsiders' medicine. You do not fear the spirits of our ancestors' gods."

"Our ancestors did not know everything."

"Silence!" the prosecutor shouted. "How dare you, a mere boy, speak against our ancestors? You have played the traitor and joined the outsiders' tribe."

An old man spoke from the circle. "The outsiders are bad. You, a chief's son, should know that. They have taken our forests, our gold, our silver, and copper."

Ramon dropped his head. He knew the elder was right. For longer than he could remember, outsiders had taken advantage of his people. The lust for gold and silver had brought the cruel Spaniards to Tarahumara territory. The Tarahumaras had left their fertile valleys and plains and fled deep into the foreboding Sierra Madre Mountains of northwestern Mexico. They had set up dwellings in caves and crude shelters. But the Spaniards had followed, forcing the able-bodied Tarahumaras to work the mines, and paying them a pittance in wages.

Then the Apaches came, swooping out of the north country, brandishing long knives, slicing off the scalps of the gentle Tarahumaras who seldom knew violence.

There were brief periods of peace, but the outsiders always came back to pirate away the timber and mineral wealth of the Tarahumara country. And the gentle Tarahumaras, uneducated and impoverished, were like clay in the brutal hands of their exploiters.

The accusing elder spoke again, more sharply. "These outsiders whom you help are worse than the others. They come to steal not only our treasure, but our customs as well."

The words raced from between Ramon's thin lips: "The Hiltons are our friends. They come to give, not to take. They offer us learning and the Book of the true God. They will help us become wise so that the bad outsiders do not cheat us."

The prosecutor shook his fist in Ramon's face. "Enough! You are a chief's son. We command you to confess your wrongs. If you do not, the birds will pick your bones while you hang from a tree."

Barely fifteen, the trembling boy slowly shook his head.

"We will give you time to think," the prosecutor said. "Go from us."

Ramon Lopez slipped away to walk the mountain trails and think—not about whether he would bend to the elders' threats and return to the customs of his ancestors, but about how he could bring a new day to his village. So long had his people walked in spiritual darkness, chained to the handed-down superstitions of their ancestors. So long had they eked out a living from the rocky ground, although the mountains were rich in mineral wealth. Ramon yearned to do something for his people, but he knew nothing could be accomplished by returning to the old ways.

A quarter century has passed since Ramon was threatened by the elders. They never made good their threats. And, through Ramon, a new day has dawned for the community of Samachique!

In the old days the Tarahumaras of Samachique lived in squalor and filth, virtual slaves to the business interests that drained the natural wealth from their mountains. The village was two and one half days' travel by mule from the nearest road. A small Mexican school functioned, but few Tarahumaras bothered to send their children. They kept them back to tend the sheep and goats and hoe the corn and squash that kept the villagers alive. Farther out in the mountains from Samachique, conditions were worse. Many country Indians lived in high caves on canyon walls. The more fortunate huddled behind crude plank shelters thrown up against boulders or the faces of cliffs.

The new day in Samachique and surrounding areas has brought a social revolution. The government school boasts five teachers and a lunchroom to feed the Indian children who must come long distances along mountain trails. A community clinic, staffed by trained nurses, is making believers in modern medicine out of the witch doctors.

A small airport is available so emergency cases can be flown out to a hospital. A good dirt road, built by a copper-mining company, leads to the outside world. A community store sells goods to residents at prices the Indians can afford.

Outside traders no longer cheat gullible, illiterate Tarahumaras. Thousands of apple trees have been planted to benefit the next generation, and the Sama-chique treasury remains full of pesos for future improvements.

All this has come from wise management of mining and timber royalties paid to the Tarahumaras by busi-ness interests. In the old days, the companies bribed Indian leaders and persuaded them to sign away the mining and timber rights for a song. Now many of the Tarahumaras can read and write and understand con-tracts.

Ramon Lopez has been the general in command of the social revolution. He was the first Tarahumara to become a member of the Chihuahua state legislature, a post he still holds. And as a member of the Supreme Tarahumara Council, he is directly responsible for the welfare of thousands of his own people.

When Ramon sits as a counselor and judge, long lines of Indians seek his counsel and arbitration of disputes. "He amazes us with his wisdom and influ-ence," says Wycliffe's Paul Carlson, who with his wife has served with the Kenneth Hiltons, the first Wy-cliffe translators to the Tarahumaras. "At first, we tried to discourage him from entering politics. We felt he could do more good as an Indian evangelist. But Ramon proved us wrong. He has remained true to the Lord and has put Christianity to work in poli-tics. He has a burning zeal to change the life of his people. But for the gospel, he could have become a Communist."

Ramon was introduced to the gospel by the Hil-

tons, who came to the Tarahumara region in 1941 to
study the unwritten language. At first the Indians
shrank from social contact with them. The Hiltons
would at times see a Tarahumara wrapped in his brown-
gray blanket approaching them on the mountain trail
ahead. Upon spying them, he would vanish among
the rugged rocks.

Previous missionaries had met with little success.
As early as 1607, the Jesuits had tried to Catholicize
the shy Indians. Father Salvatierra, a man who came
in 1684, became terrified on the narrow trail and slid
off his horse opposite the precipice.

Over the years the Jesuits kept up sporadic efforts,
although there was one lapse of 130 years. The Tarahumaras suffered greatly between the seventeenth
and twentieth centuries; from the Spaniards, from
raiding Apaches, and from crafty traders and business-
men who separated the illiterate Indians from their
natural resources.

Conditions became so bad that in 1924 an armed
Mexican official invaded the Baptist church in Chihuahua City, two hundred miles away, and demanded
that the church members do something about the
exploiting of the Tarahumaras. The aroused congregation sent their pastor, Mateo M. Gurrola, to preach
and distribute Spanish literature among the Tarahumaras. This accomplished little, for few of the
Indians could even read the Spanish alphabet.

Two years later the evangelical Methodists tried to

establish a mission foothold, but were also confounded by the language problem.

The first language expert visited the Tarahumaras in 1936 and surveyed the possibilities of writing down the language for Scripture translation. This was Eugene Nida, who is presently Translation Secretary of the American Bible Society.

Nine years later the Hiltons and their four children rode in by horseback over the precipitous trails to become the first resident Bible translators. The Wycliffe group had been officially organized only three years before. One of their first friends was Ramon Lopez, the chief's son, who had learned to read and write and speak Spanish in the village school. Ramon became Kenneth Hilton's indispensable language helper in recording the strange sounds.

For hours on end, Kenneth Hilton and Ramon sat compiling the symbols of Tarahumara sounds on stacks of three-by-five-inch pieces of paper. Ramon patiently repeated sounds of Tarahumara words over and over until the translator was certain he had the words phonetically correct. One word, *chabochi,* gave Hilton a hint of how the Tarahumaras viewed outsiders. The word referred both to an outsider and a yellow spider!

Soon after beginning the language work, Ramon confessed faith in Christ. This surprised the Hiltons, for the Tarahumaras believed they alone were children of God and that all outsiders were aliens. When questioned about his faith, Ramon said, "My grandparents prepared me to believe. They did not know about Jesus, but they loved God and taught me that I should obey Him."

Ramon's boyhood friend, Felix, also professed faith. But when persecution descended, he shrank back, leaving Ramon to stand alone in the tribe for many years.

Ramon's faith underwent severe testing from many quarters. The tribal council of elders publicly rebuked and threatened him, and boys his age treated him as an outsider. A serious illness plagued him during his late teen years. But the greatest trial came when his young wife and baby died a short time apart.

Kenneth Hilton tried to comfort his young Timothy. "God is not against you, Ramon," he assured. "He does not punish Christians with illness. He wishes to be your Companion and Guide."

"See, the spirits are punishing you," the medicine men taunted. "This is because you have taken the outsiders' religion." The witch doctors believed that evil spirits were everywhere, especially beside still mountain pools. Later, when the translators sought to put the Twenty-third Psalm into Tarahumara, they had to use a symbol other than "beside still waters" to depict the spiritual life.

The Hiltons sent repeated requests for prayer to friends in the United States. In December, 1950, they reported:

> He is a long-suffering and merciful God, not willing that any should perish, ever longing for all to come

to repentance. Here among the Tarahumaras we still see no longing on their part. Ramon continues joyfully faithful though others are not concerned. The translation of John's Gospel is now proceeding into the last chapter. Distribution of the printed copies of Mark is slow because of the high percentage of illiteracy. The people are as apathetic toward learning to read as they are toward hearing the Word of God.

The central office of the Wycliffe Bible Translators in California issued a special call for prayer: "Let us join the Hiltons in praying that the Lord will create in the hearts of the Tarahumaras a real hunger for His Word."

Finally the seed sown in nine years of patient missionary work began to sprout, and here and there a green blade of spiritual response sprang up. For the first time, Tarahumaras in small groups began gathering to hear Ramon and Kenneth Hilton teach the Scriptures.

The second translation team arrived in 1951: Paul and Ellen Carlson and their three children. Paul Carlson had been a wrestling champion at Wheaton College and later worked in research for a missile firm. He had also studied electronics at Harvard and the Massachusetts Institute of Technology and had first offered his scientific talents to the Wycliffe organization. But at the Wycliffe school of linguistics, held at the University of Oklahoma, he felt God wanted him to help in translation work.

The Carlsons built their home out of volcanic stone and began conducting campfire socials. The shy Indians came out of their crude homes and actually seemed to enjoy the games and singing. Ellen Carlson used her sewing machine to attract the women who for centuries had made their garments by hand. Now here was a magical way of making clothing.

The Tarahumara church had taken root under the ministry of the Hiltons and now, with the reinforcement of the Carlsons, the visible congregation began to materialize. Not by large numbers, but by one and two at a time did the believers come forth.

Ramon, who remarried and began raising a second family, continued as the leader of the Tarahumara church. He began participating in the negotiations between the business interests and the Tarahumaras and showed the ability to drive a hard bargain.

With increased royalties from the companies, the life of the Tarahumaras in and around Samachique began taking a new twist. The school system was enlarged with lessons in both Spanish and Tarahumara. The printed gospel of Mark, which had been translated by the Hiltons, was used for reading material. Wages also increased as the Indians worked harder and applied new skills to their jobs. Many community facilities were added.

Today the town of Samachique is a showplace as the result of indigenous missionary work and education. The National Indian Institute of Mexico cooperates with the translators, Ramon, and other Indian leaders to improve living conditions. A new railroad, boasting twenty-four bridges and seventy-three tunnels, has opened up more remote areas of the Tarahumara region.

A third Wycliffe couple recently began work among the Tarahumaras: Don and Esther Burgess. Esther, the daughter of the Carlsons and a graduate of Stanford University, is one of several second-generation Wycliffe members now pioneering for Christ.

Don Burgess, like his father-in-law, was a college athlete. He was captain of the basketball team at Texas Western University and met the Carlsons while working on a summer railroad job in the state of Chihuahua. A Mexican engineer suggested that Paul should meet "another gringo who doesn't drink." Don was introduced to Paul Carlson and the missionary invited him to visit their home in Samachique. There Don met Esther, one of the Carlsons' daughters. They fell in love, married, and joined Wycliffe.

"We've already begun work in another Tarahumara dialect spoken farther back in the mountains," Don says. "Some of these Indians live on bare ground and hunt only with bow and arrows. They have never heard about Jesus, and we hope to tell them about Him in their own language."

The Carlsons are now on leave of absence, and the Hiltons are continuing work in the Samachique region. The Hiltons are not discouraged by the slow growth of the Tarahumara church. "The present believers will help win their fellow tribesmen. Soon, for the first time, more than 40,000 Tarahumara Indians will have the New Testament in their own language," translator Hilton notes.

Speaking about his hard-to-reach people, Ramon Lopez asks, "Do you wonder why the seed of God's Word sown among the Tarahumaras has been slow to sprout? We were always taught by the old ones that outsiders were children of the devil, black spiders. When these 'outsiders' came to talk to us about the true God it seemed impossible that they could have anything to teach us—we, who called ourselves 'sons of God.' But now we know better."

J.C.H.

8

Tell Us Where God Lives

THE MULE SNORTED, kicked up his hind legs like an oversized jack rabbit, and bolted into the tall Mexican pines. Nicolas, like a true Huisteco Indian, curled his thin lips and spat an acid curse at the fleeing maverick.

Martin, Nick's father-in-law, a short, thick man with a whimsical smile riveted to his deeply lined face, yelled for Nick to stop the mule.

"We can't make liquor without sugarcane," he called.

Confident in Nick's ability to retrieve the mule, Martin walked on through the pines to a large clearing to wait.

The clearing was notable because it marked the entrance to Huisteco Indian territory, and because of a large, rugged wooden cross which stood there. Travelers coming and going from the market in Las Casas always stopped, doffed their hats, and bowed in devout reverence at this holy place.

Before Martin reached the correct place to remove his hat, he noticed a Tzeltal Indian walking up the trail from the opposite side. To Martin's amazement, the Tzeltal walked past the cross without bowing or removing his hat.

How strange, he thought, *that the Tzeltal doesn't bow down to our holy cross. I will question him about this.*

"How are you?" said Martin to the Tzeltal. "Where are you going?"

In noncommital Indian fashion, the Tzeltal answered that he was fine and that he wasn't going anywhere.

Martin stood silent for a moment, then reached into his woven palm bag and pulled out a pack of cigarettes and offered them to the man in front of him.

"Thank you," said the Tzeltal, "but I don't smoke or drink anymore because I now know where God is."

"Oh?" questioned Martin. "I always thought God lived in the cross and in the church."

"No," replied the Tzeltal in a serious voice. "He lives in heaven and in men's hearts."

"Your words interest me," Martin mused. "Why don't you come back to my house where we can talk. I would like my son-in-law to hear as well."

"Listen," answered the Tzeltal, "I have walked seven hours from my village and I am now only one hour from the Las Casas market. Let me complete my buying first, and in the morning I will gladly visit you."

I wonder, thought the Tzeltal as he made his way down the narrow, dry path, *if the Huisteco lies as usual and uses this as an excuse to ambush me. Would it be that God could work in their drunken hearts? How often have my Christian brothers witnessed to the proud Huisteco and not one has ever believed.*

It was still dark when the Tzeltal arrived the next morning at the arranged meeting place on the top of a long hill. He cupped his hands to his mouth and called into the cold, predawn darkness, his voice echoing down the hill into the canyon. For a moment all was silent except for the soft wind humming through the pines. Then, like a forest shadow, Martin appeared from behind a large bush where he had waited throughout the night.

"Where's your son-in-law?" asked the Tzeltal nervously.

"He waits with the mules in the cornfields below," answered Martin. "Come, I have sent word to my relatives that you will tell us where God lives."

Twenty Huistecos waited silently in front of Martin's split-cedar shake house.

When the three men walked into Martin's front yard, the Tzeltal noticed four large brewing vats full of liquor. "That stuff's no good," he said firmly. "We Tzeltals used to fight and kill each other when we got drunk. You should believe on the Lord and throw this stuff away."

The Huistecos sat and grinned at the Tzeltal. The

idea of throwing good liquor away was highly amusing to the materialistic Huisteco mind.

The Tzeltal then explained how he had personally come to understand how God loved him. He spoke with such firm sincerity and honesty that each Huisteco soon found his grin replaced with a pensive frown as he thought about the words he had just heard.

After the Tzeltal's testimony, Martin and his relatives, in Huisteco fashion, discussed the man's words. At length, Martin spoke, "You are from another tribe. We Huistecos never believe outsiders. But this is good what we hear. We will believe! We have always wanted a living person who would save us. Isn't that true, Nicolas?"

"If you and Nicolas want to believe," said the Tzeltal excitedly, "I will bring others to talk and play records for you. When you hear the words from God's Book in your own language, it will help you to understand better."

Without waiting to hear further comments, the Tzeltal excused himself and started out over the trail for his village of Corralito. So high was his excitement over the Huistecos wanting to believe, he ran the eight hours to his village.

The following Sunday the Tzeltal stood at the front of his mud-walled church and told his story. When he asked for volunteers to go to the Huistecos and play records, three men immediately shot up their hands.

The next week the men from the church went to Martin's house, played the records, and then invited

Nick and Martin back to Corralito for a Christmas fiesta.

"How can you be sure they won't eat us if we go?" said Nick anxiously.

"Ah," said Martin, trying to sound unconcerned, "it's women's talk that Evangelicals eat people."

The two men accepted the invitation. But, standing at the foot of the long hill leading up to the Tzeltal village, Nick wondered if he and Martin hadn't accepted too hastily.

"Look," said Martin, "there are just four men and a girl coming to meet us. What can they do?"

But as Nick and Martin came to the top of the hill they stopped short in their tracks. A cold prickly fear raced up their backs.

A huge crowd of Tzeltal believers who had gathered for their fiesta, turned and looked in silence at the Huistecos. It seemed to Nick and Martin that each of the large metal cooking pots was bubbling just for them! "Oh no-o-o," said Nick as he looked at Martin with a what-do-we-do-now expression.

Before Martin could answer, the Tzeltals called a cheery welcome to the new arrivals, raced up, shook their hands warmly, and invited them to eat. They prefaced each greeting with "Believe on the Lord."

It was soon apparent to Nick and Martin that the Tzeltals meant only goodwill. They were especially astonished that since they were strangers the Tzeltals would share food with them without charging them for it.

"We do this because we know God lives in our hearts," the Tzeltal explained when Nick asked why.

Thirteen years have now passed since Nick stood around that Tzeltal campfire wondering if he would ever leave the village alive. But he did leave, weak at first in his new faith and desperately trying to understand this new change that had taken over his mind and heart.

Nick's wife, bewildered by his sudden and unprecedented action of refusing to drink with his friends, accused him of losing his manhood.

For months Nick stood alone. At first his father-in-law, Martin, showed signs of growing, but the power of ridicule, isolation and fear caused him to join his drinking cronies again. When Nick stubbornly refused to join the crowd, the townspeople threatened to burn his house and kill him.

"What right have you to choose a life different from the rest of us?" taunted the village elders.

At night, Nick's mind was beseiged with uncontrollable nightmares. Every unfamiliar noise made his heart sink. *Is it tonight?* he wondered. *Is this the night they will come to kill me?*

When he met Tzeltal believers on the trail to question them about the Scriptures, Nick often told them about his fear. "How can I be a believer if I am so frightened?" he would ask. With a knowing understanding of similar pain, the Tzeltal Christians prayed with Nick and lovingly encouraged him in his new faith.

One day he witnessed to two young brothers on the trail. "Your words sound good," they said. "We will believe." Returning to their home, they immediately threw out their wooden idols.

"What have you done to the idols?" demanded their father when he returned from the cornfield.

"We now know," they said enthusiastically, "that these idols of wood are not real. The true God is in heaven and will live in your heart if you ask him. Why don't you believe too?"

He did. And when Nick preached at the old man's funeral several years later, five sons and three daughters stood around his coffin to sing praise to the living God they had each come to know intimately.

The effect on Nick was like being in a dark room and opening the door into sunlight. His fears vanished and his faith became rock-hard.

And, because of that faith, in future years a school and a clinic became a reality for the Huistecos.

"Nick is like a modern Paul to his own people," says Marion Cowan, the Wycliffe translator living in the valley. "Of the 250 Huisteco believers, almost all have been won to the Lord directly through listening to Nick and observing his life."

H.S.

9

Domingo and the Fakers

DOMINGO PAULINO kicked stones down the steep mountainside as he waited for the chattering witch doctors to catch up. As a policeman in his Eastern Otomi* Indian village of San Antonio in a remote region of Central Mexico, he had been assigned to escort the medicine men on their pilgrimage to a sacred house in the woods.

He started to yell at the leader to hurry along, but choked off the sound at second thought. Lately he had become suspicious of the witch doctors. "Big wind—no rain," he had told a sick friend who had not been helped by the witch doctor's incantations.

Domingo had never doubted their power before. Many times he had watched them cut out paper figures and place them on sick people. But recently some of the witch doctors had been sneaking around to Arti and Cata's house to get stuck by the needle and take pills. Domingo knew—he had seen them.

*Eastern Otomi and Mesquital Otomi are related dialects but mutually unintelligible.

Arti and Cata were the two Bible translators who had recently come to Santiago. Arti was dark-haired and a Mexican with sparkling eyes from Mexico City. Cata was brunette and from the big country to the north. Cata and another foreigner had first come to Domingo's father's house. Domingo remembered the visit for he was there.

"Papa!" he had shouted. "Two foreign women are coming up the trail."

His father had hurried across the dirt floor of their hut and peered through the opening that served for a door.

The strangers shouted their greetings in Otomi while Domingo and his brothers pranced around their father. Cata and her companion, Viola, quickly introduced themselves and announced the reason for their visit. "We heard, Señor Paulino, that you have the Book of God. We would like to teach your family from it."

Domingo recalled how his father's eyes had flashed as he motioned for one of the children to get the big book. "It is Spanish," he told the strangers. "I bought it many moons ago. We speak only Otomi."

The strangers merely smiled and pointed across a range of mountains. "Beyond there," Cata said in plain Otomi, "live other Otomis who speak your tongue. We have been studying with them and learning to write your words. Now we have come to your village to learn more and to put God's sayings in

Otomi. We want to teach both young and old to read God's sayings."

The father welcomed them, and his older son, Juan, built them a hut. Then Viola went to another village when another translator, Arti, arrived. Arti and Cata stayed on to study and teach from God's sayings.

The voice of the lead witch doctor jolted Domingo from his thoughts. "On, policeman! We must give offerings before sunset."

Domingo glared at the waspish little man and started moving again. As he climbed, he kept thinking of what he had learned in Cata and Arti's hut. "There is only one true God," Cata had said. "We should worship Him, not the things He has made. He has sent His Son to forgive your bad deeds."

The procession reached the sacred house and Domingo stood aside to let the witch doctors pass into the sacred hut with the offerings they were bringing to the gods of earth, fire and water.

Domingo peered after them. He wanted very much to go inside. All his life he had heard that the spirits of dead witch doctors talked in the house. "We have been there," the village elders had said. "They talk from behind the *petate* that divides the house."

Domingo crept to the entrance. He heard talking inside. Familiar voices. Could it be? On impulse Domingo stepped inside. A witch doctor frowned at him, but he remained.

The voices were coming from behind the *petate* mat that hung from the grass roof.

Suddenly Domingo stepped up to the *petate* and peeked around. His fear turned to disgust as he saw only some friends of the witch doctors sitting there. They were the "spirits" he had heard.

Domingo stamped the dirt floor with his sandaled feet, thinking, *If the witch doctors have lied about this house, they have deceived us about other things.*

He left them and climbed to a sacred cave high on the mountainside where witch doctors placed offerings. They had warned that anyone trying to enter the cave would fall to his death or be bitten by deadly snakes. Was this another example of fakery?

He peered inside the smoky interior. There was not a single snake!

"If the witch doctors are wrong," he muttered, "Cata and Arti must be right." Domingo swallowed hard. To follow in their way, he knew, would mean no more drinking. He loved to drink the native corn liquor and strut about in the village. "No!" he almost shouted aloud. "The foreigners' way is not for me."

* * *

The annual village fiesta came with much drinking, dancing and feasting. Domingo made a liquor barrel of his stomach and swaggered and joked until his head reeled. Then he crawled into the woods and fell asleep.

He awoke to feel rain pouring on his bare chest.

"I am the village policeman," he growled at himself, "and I have played the fool."

It was several days before he could bring himself to go to the Bible women. He found Cata talking to his father about Nicodemus' interview with Jesus. Domingo squatted on the floor and listened thoughtfully.

Later that day, Domingo knocked at the door of the new house which his older brother had built for Cata and Arti.

"Teach me from God's Book," he asked. "Tell me about Nicodemus and God's Son."

Cata Voigtlander repeated the Bible story several times for Domingo. He kept asking, "How can I be born again? I was born once, no?"

"You must turn away from the false gods and ask God's forgiveness," she said. "You must believe that His Son will forgive you."

Domingo nodded his dark head. "I will think about this. Tonight I will come back."

Later Domingo joined other villagers who had gathered in the house for evening Bible study. He stood up and asked to speak. "I have been on the wrong way," he said. "But I have asked God to forgive my sins. I believe in His Son—here." He thumped his chest to emphasize his testimony.

He kept coming to the meetings regularly and listened to the New Testament passages read in his own language. He also served as a language helper for the translators. Then Cata told him that she and Arti

were needed in Mexico City to help prepare some
new books for printing. "We will return soon," she
told Domingo. "While we are away, tell your friends
what we have told you from God's Book."

Cata and Arti walked to a neighboring town where
they were picked up by a small plane and flown
into the capital. Cata had been an artist before joining
Wycliffe and her talents were needed in preparing
some new primers and translations in other languages
for publication. Several weeks later, she and Arti
were surprised by the arrival of Domingo and three
friends.

"We've told the people all we know," Domingo
said. "Now, we would like to learn more."

"Where will they stay?" Cata asked Arti. "Our
Wycliffe quarters are full."

Arti solved this problem by housing the four young
Otomi men in her father's garage. Both Cata and Arti
took time out from their duties to work on the New
Testament translations with Domingo and his friends.
Finally, the Indians left for their village, happy with
their hoard of new knowledge.

When Arti and Cata returned to San Antonio, they
found that Domingo had turned his small home into
a chapel. Nearby he had built another hut for his
family to occupy. Five nights each week he and other
Christian men were leading Bible studies.

Now a growing evangelical church in San Antonio
is led by Domingo. The translators have published
Mark, Acts, John, James, and the epistles of John

in the dialect and are pushing toward the goal of publishing the entire New Testament in Eastern Otomi.

But Domingo has become restless. "There are many other villages out in the mountains," he told Cata and Arti. "The people still believe the witch doctors. We must hurry God's Word to them."

J.C.H.

10

The Church in Tomato Gulch

OUR TINY PIPER CUB seemed to be at the mercy of the rising air currents almost as soon as we took off from the Missionary Aviation Fellowship base in the state of Oaxaca. Strong winds had blown thick cushions of gleaming white clouds over the mountains so that the peaks looked like castle spires rising from downy beds of celestial foam.

It wasn't long before all thought of grandeur left me—along with my breakfast! Without warning, our pilot plummeted us onto a postage-stamp-size airstrip set at a thirty-five-degree angle on top of a bald mountain. I staggered out into the friendly smiles of fifty assorted Chinantec believers.

We had arrived at Tomato Gulch, a tiny village in southeastern Mexico, six hundred feet above sea level in a tropical rain forest. This Indian village interested me for two reasons: first, because a strong healthy church had quickly sprouted after the gospel was planted; second, because the church in its infancy was battered and bruised by severe persecution. I wanted to find out what made this church strong.

Walking down from the airstrip, I asked Calvin Rensch, resident translator in this area, how his work was progressing.

"Incredibly," he said. "The believers are growing stronger every day. On their own initiative, without my help or suggestion, they elected elders and chose the 'one who would make the Scriptures plain.' Some of the elders chosen were ones I would not have selected, but they know their people much better than I."

Cal went on to say that a man from another sect had come through their area trying to win over the Christian believers. He told them, among other things, that they should not drink coffee or water with their tortillas. A believer from another area heard about this and walked five hours over the trail to the town of Tomato Gulch. When he arrived he told the brethren, "I have come to fix up your hearts." He simply meant he was going to give them some proper instruction from the Word of God.

"What new things have happened since the gospel came to your people?" I asked.

"Well, for one thing," Cal said, "the believers help each other as they never did before. When a house is to be built, the brethren will gather ridgepoles and balsa stripping to lace the poles together. They help in the heavy work of digging post holes and dragging grass and palm from the hills. The believers have become deeply aware of each other's needs, something that is foreign to past Chinantec culture. Before, a Chinantec could eat in front of a man who might literally be starving, and he would never be bothered by conscience.

"The Christians have also learned to sing," Cal added. Before, only drunks sang.

"When believers saw me pray and read the Scriptures with my family after breakfast, they became concerned about having their own set time each day to read and pray. Some have now established a regular practice of family worship all on their own initiative."

What effects had the believers had on other members of the tribe? Cal said that in one village, forty-five minutes' walk from Tomato Gulch, the opposition came one night and removed the images from the local Catholic church. There were so many Christians in the village that they feared the idols would not be cared for.

From where we sat on the stone porch of Cal's house I could see the town jail, a stone-block building with a heavy wooden lattice door that kept prisoners cramped in a six-by-nine-foot space.

"I remember the circumstances that led up to our believers being thrown in jail," Cal recalled. "I had translated the gospel of Mark and would read and explain the Scriptures to seven fellows who came to our house every night. I knew their families and friends were pressuring them not to come, but they came anyway. The Word of God in their own Chinantec language fascinated them.

"After they decided to 'grab hold of the Word' [the idiom for believing] they were threatened with expulsion from the tribe. The town elders were furious because the new Christians would not play in the band for fiestas that honored images. The fiesta season is the worst time of year for corruption of every kind, and the new Christians wanted no part of their old life. The elders were upset because the new believers were no longer following the ways of their ancestors.

"The local townspeople made the fellows use the back mountain trails. This is no small feat. The trails are almost perpendicular! When the town elders saw that the believers meant business, they made the local store off limits. They told one Christian that he could no longer live in his house and threatened to kill him if he continued in the 'new way.'

"When the seven men began witnessing to other Chinantecs and holding Bible studies in each other's homes, the authorities decided to act. Ironically, the elders came to me for help.

" 'We need a chain and lock for the jail door,' they said.

"I gave them a padlock and chain. I didn't find out until the next morning that I had played a part in putting the believers behind bars!

"The believers were kept there for three days. Passersby would taunt the fellows with 'Why doesn't your new God come down and let you out?' or 'Who made you so smart to change from our tribal traditions?' When the fellows were released it was with further threats of being killed and with warnings not to continue in the new way.

" 'How could we do anything else but continue following God?' John Bighorn said to me. 'The clear words of God in my own Chinantec language have shown me the road so much better.'

"Another told me later, 'I thank God that He gave His Son who shows us the path so we can see clearly. I have now become a mature man.'

"Even after their church was burned to ashes they said, 'We will not turn back! The gospel is like a cool refreshing drink of water after we have worked all day in the cornfield.' "

Cal and his wife, Carolyn, arrived in Chinantec country in 1956. The Indians, not knowing what to do, gave them a community hut in which to live. The Rensches' strange food and even stranger way of cooking made happy amusement for everyone. Cal and Carolyn worked among them good-naturedly, treating their infected insect and snake bites, and dispensing pills to relieve the strength-sapping problems of hookworm and a multitude of other intestinal parasites. Through showing kindness and through their ability in learning to speak the difficult Chinantec language, they were able to learn the tribal culture and thought patterns.

Sitting outside under the blinking Southern Cross, Cal listened to the men tell stories of ancient folklore, heard their fears, their dreams and hopes. Because there was communication in language and culture, with the Renches identifying themselves with the Chinantecs in every way, the missionaries' ultimate ministry of translating the New Testament into the Chinatec language started out on solid ground. The proof was plain to see.

One Monday night I watched from behind an overcrowded medical counter as twelve men hunched around Cal. He explained the words that were typed on sheets of bond paper. These were the Scripture portions to be used in the worship service on the following Sunday. Cal told me later that these men simply had to "scoop" the other believers in finding out what the Scriptures were saying.

From a hill overlooking a smooth jungle stream, I saw a thatched building. A line of Chinantec men in sun-bleached shirts passed through a low door on one end. Soon, above the deep whisper of wind through the thick jungle trees, I heard singing. The language I did not understand, but the tune was unmistakably "Near to the Heart of God." As I sloshed my way through the river I heard a different tune, hauntingly beautiful. "That," said Cal, "is a song one of our Chinantec believers composed. It has become a favorite among the eleven congregations.

"There are now more than 350 believers in eleven

villages," he continued, "and each week I am introduced to new people who have decided to 'grab hold' of the Word of God.

"The Chinantec church decided that they should be responsible for witnessing and reaching their own people. My job, they said, was to bring them more and more of the Word of God. The Scriptures in their own language have become meaningful to the Chinantecs. For years they have slipped and slid on the road of despair and fear. The gospel has given them a deep sense of belonging.

"They have also come to understand, through reading the Scriptures, that they have a responsibility beyond their own tribe. Six months ago they heard about a group of Indian believers in another part of Mexico who had been driven from their land and were without food and shelter. The Chinantec church collected $3.60 and sent it as an offering to help this persecuted group."

The Chinantec church is barely five years old. Yet, armed with parts of the New Testament in their own language, they have come to understand that their directive force is Christ and their basic principle is love. They have "become mature men, reaching to the very height of Christ's full stature" (Eph 4:13, TEV).

H.S.

11

Totonac Treasure

I CLOSE MY EYES and say, "Have I been dreaming?" I open them and know that what has been happening is true. I, Manuel Arenas, who once lived in primitive darkness am a Christian and a university graduate. I have traveled throughout Europe and North America and can speak four languages. This is all so wonderful—so miraculous. God must have all the credit for bringing me out of darkness.

No one knows how long Totonacs have lived in the Mexican states of Vera Cruz and Puebla. Cortez tricked my ancestors into helping the Spaniards defeat the Aztec nation. Then he made the Totonacs his slaves. To this day, Totonacs are suspicious of foreigners.

My people still live much as they did when Cortez arrived. They plant corn and beans on steep mountainsides with the primitive dibble stick. They eat and sleep on earthen floors in thatch huts and follow customs handed down for centuries. Except for Mexican traders, little influence has filtered in from the outside world. Our language is the biggest barrier. It was never written down until the American came, which is where my story must begin.

Herman Aschmann was soaking wet from two days of trudging muddy trails when he walked into my village of San Felipe Tecpatlan. He was given a room behind the village saloon where he began learning our difficult language. Noisy drunks interfered with his study so he moved into the jail. It was conveniently next door to the school, and the translator learned Totonac words from the children. Later he married Bessie Dawson, another Wycliffe Bible Translator, and built his own house.

I was only eight when Herman came in 1940. How I wanted to be his language helper. But he chose another Totonac boy named Fortensio who was very smart. I hung around his house and, when a tragic accident happened, I got my chance.

Poor Fortensio was working in his father's steep cornfield when he lost his balance and fell, landing on a sharp boulder. He died soon afterward and Herman asked me to help him.

Herman offered me pay. I refused. Just to study with the educated and kindly American was reward enough. As we worked on the language together, I stole glances at his books on a shelf and dreamed of being able to read them.

Soon I was helping Herman translate the New Testament. This was all very new and strange to me.

My mother had always taught me that our Totonac idols were real gods.

One day my friend read to me in Totonac, "For God so loved the world, that he gave his only begotten Son, that whosoever believeth in him should not perish, but have everlasting life."

He asked if I was a Christian and I replied, "Of course. Do you think I am an animal?" Ever since the Spanish conquest, Totonacs have believed that anyone who is not an animal is a Christian.

Then Herman explained what it meant to believe in Jesus Christ as the Saviour of the world. I wanted to believe in Jesus, but first I had to make a test.

I sneaked my mother's biggest sewing needle and went straight to an idol. I said, "If I stick this needle into the idol's foot and blood comes out I will know the idol is a god. If not, I will believe what Herman said about Jesus."

I jabbed the needle into the idol. No blood came out. "He's right," I said, and not long after that I truly gave my life to Jesus Christ and promised I would serve Him wherever He wanted me.

My father noticed I was spending more and more time with the Aschmanns. First he said, "You're lazy. You don't want to work in the fields, so you go to the foreigners' house." But when he discovered I trusted in Jesus instead of the idol gods, he gave me thirty minutes to come back to the old gods or pack all my things and leave.

"Father," I said, "you are asking me to choose between two religions. I cannot give up that which is not a religion but a Person, the Lord Jesus Christ. He lives in my heart."

But my father was adamant and made me leave. Later when I tried to return, he burned all my belongings.

The Aschmanns took me in and Herman and I continued working on the Bible translation. It was hard work for we had no dictionaries or grammars to consult when we got stuck. Often I was tempted to quit and go work on a farm or in Mexico City as some of my friends were doing. But then I would think of how badly my people needed the Word of God in the Totonac language and I would continue working.

Finally after nine years we finished the New Testament translation. After it was printed by the American Bible Society, a Mexico City television station invited us to appear on a program and talk about the translation. I held up a copy and said, "This is the New Testament in my Totonac language. It is big because our Totonac language words are long—like Turkish words."

A Turkish doctor saw me and called the headquarters of the Wycliffe Bible Translators. He asked if I would come and show him the New Testament. I visited the doctor in Mexico City's best section. Later he accepted Christ.

God had already impressed me that I should become educated and help my people. Several hundred

Totonacs had become believers in Jesus. Few could read or write.

I started to night school in Mexico City, working by day to support myself. First I swept out saloons—the only job I could get. Later I worked as kitchen and yard boy for the Wycliffe Translators, and as a messenger for a Mexican army general.

The general flew me to New York where we stayed at the Waldorf-Astoria. He wanted to send me to General Electric for special training, but I was afraid I might get swallowed up by the desire to make money and live in luxury. I thanked him and declined.

After finishing high school in Mexico City, I rode a bus to the United States border at Juárez. But the customs officials refused to let me enter. They said I had to have three hundred American dollars. I had only seventy-five Mexican pesos—about six dollars.

As I was walking away, an old woman spoke to me. "Manuel, do you not remember me? I'm Armando's mother." I remembered. I had met her son, a pilot, in Mexico City. "He's at the airport now and would be glad to see you," she added.

I took a taxi to the airport. Armando asked me what I was doing at the border and I explained my problem. He gave me a check for four hundred dollars for which I thanked him and the Lord.

In Los Angeles I met a Christian businessman who paid my fare to the Prairie Bible Institute in Three Hills, Alberta. I studied there awhile, then chest injuries from an automobile accident made it necessary for me to return to Mexico. When I recovered, I went to the University of Chicago. Working and going to school became too much for me; I had to be hospitalized. When I got the four hundred dollar hospital bill, I was ready to give up and return to Mexico. Then a doctor told me, "A friend of yours has paid the bill." Right there I resolved never to complain again about the Lord's dealings.

The University of Chicago required me to take one foreign language. Since I could already speak Spanish, I decided to study German. At that time I didn't know why.

I applied for a scholarship in Germany, then returned to Mexico City for a visit. While there I fell and damaged several vertebrae. I had to wear a cast for several weeks and lie with my face downward, not able to even wash my hands and face. Herman lovingly did this chore for me. I continued practicing my German, hopeful that the scholarship would come through.

After a while I could walk a block or two outdoors. On one of my walks my shoes came untied. A policeman saw that I could not bend down, and tied them for me. I thanked him with a peso and a gospel tract. The policeman read the tract and asked for more.

"It is the last I have," I said, "but I will be glad to talk to you more."

We went to a restaurant and over coffee I explained the way of salvation more fully. The policeman trusted in Christ.

We exchanged names but did not see each other for several months. When we again met near a police station, the policeman said, "Please wait here five minutes." He brought back five other officers and I wondered, *Why would six policemen be coming for me?* I soon found out. My friend explained that he had talked to them and all had accepted Christ as their Saviour.

Good news came that my German scholarship application had been accepted. Then I knew God had led me to study German at the University of Chicago. As soon as possible I left for Erlangen University.

In Germany I met many new friends. They invited me to speak in their churches and asked me many questions about the Totonacs. A little girl overheard me telling about the need for a Bible school for the Totonacs and handed me four marks. "I've been saving for a new doll," she said, "but I want to give it for the Totonac Bible School." I almost cried.

When I received my degree, I was offered a fine teaching position. "No," I said, "I must go back and teach my people, the Totonacs."

On my way home I stopped off at New York to help with the Wycliffe exhibit at the World's Fair. Again I had trouble at customs. The officers were suspicious of my Mexican passport because it had so many marks of entry to East Germany. They cleared me after I explained I had made these trips to take Bibles to Christian friends in the Communist zone.

When the World's Fair closed I returned to Mexico

and started a Bible school for the Totonacs. There are now Christian congregations in eight villages. The largest has over five hundred members and is self-supporting. Two native preachers have been installed as pastors and several other young men want to study.

I am often asked, "Why don't young Totonacs go to Spanish-speaking schools?" Of course they do for elementary education. But Totonacs do not truly understand Spanish sermons. When I am among my people, I always speak to them in Totonac. They understand the language of our fathers.

Over 100,000 speak Totonac in Mexico. It is an awkward language to English speakers because our long words are made of many prefixes and suffixes. Some English sentences can be put into one Totonac word.

Our Totonac school includes a farm and low-cost housing. Students must bring their families and live at the school. We teach Bible, sermon preparation, better farming, carpentering, tailoring, and other trades. Most Totonac preachers must support their families.

Our progressive Mexican government is pushing ahead in education and vocational training. Modern civilization is advancing on the Totonacs. Being a Christian, I know that technology and civilized luxuries are not enough. My people who are still in darkness need the light of God's Word. I thank God for sending Herman and Bessie Aschmann to teach me the gospel and translate the New Testament. Now

I must help other Totonac Christians extend the light they have brought.

As told to J.C.H.

12

Three Who Came Back

THE THREE TOTONAC INDIAN WOMEN carefully wound their long, thick, colorful braids over their heads and began descending the slippery riverbank. They had not bothered to pull up their braids on the six previous crossings, but here the water was deeper and they wanted to look their best when they arrived in the "big city" of Poza Rica, Mexico, which was only two more river crossings away. Their excitement at visiting the city for the first time was like that of small children at a party.

The two-day hike through the lush humid jungle of southern Veracruz, Mexico, had been wonderfully pleasant. Wild orchids splashed brilliant shades of yellows, reds, and blues against the intense greenery along the jungle trail.

Occasionally the women's conversation would be interrupted by the excited chatter of a busy red-top woodpecker searching for his noonday meal. Now and then a beak-heavy toucan would lift himself to a higher branch to scrutinize the three women more carefully.

Their excitement was heightened as they realized that soon they would be seeing the oil wells of the coastal city of Poza Rica for the first time. Ever since word reached their village of Chicontla about the *petroleros'* strange new structures on the coast, they had had a great desire to see them.

There was also excited talk of the extra things they could buy with the fifteen-peso-a-day wages they would receive in the city—more than twice the amount they could earn in their village. Also there would be extra money from the sale of the vanilla pods they were carrying to sell at one of the local hotel restaurants.

At the hotel where they sold their vanilla, the manager showed them a book which he said was written in their own Totonac language.

"Impossible," they said. "It is not possible that a book could be written in our language. We have always been told that the only books in the world were in Spanish."

"But, señoras," the hotel clerk pleaded, "these are truly books in your language. In fact, this is not just any book; this is the New Testament in Totonac. An American, Don Pedro Aschmann, left these here with me to sell. Why don't you buy a New Testament with the money I gave you for your vanilla and read for yourself what God's Word sounds like in Totonac? I, too, speak Totonac, though I'm from a different village than yours, but to me these words sound just the way God would have spoken to us."

The three women carefully counted out the thirteen one-peso bills and fifty centavos (about $1.10 in U.S. money) and went out.

A great gas pipe raised itself above the horizon ahead of the women like a skinny dragon spewing its amber tongue of flame and smoke against the darkening sky, turning the seventy-five oil derricks into angular skeletons of some strange prehistoric monsters.

All this was lost to the women. They could hardly contain their emotions—a book in their own language! "How wonderful!" they said to each other. The book so captivated them, they hardly noticed the attractions of the city's mechanization.

The women had become so excited upon finding the book that they almost forgot that none of them could read it. The hotel clerk had said, "Why don't you take the book and read it and see for yourselves?" As they recalled his words, the bitter truth of their inability to read suddenly quenched their elation.

As they walked along, however, a ray of hope flashed into their minds: Would it be possible for three women to learn to read at their age?

"Why not?" said one of them. "My daughter Chela knows how to read. She is a girl—a woman, and if she can read, we can too! We will ask her to teach us how to read, also, so that we can read for ourselves what God is saying in His Book!"

Weeks turned into months as Chela, the daughter of one of the three women, with characteristic Indian patience gave reading lessons to her mother and her two friends. Finally the three pupils began to read from their precious new Book. For seven years they had heard the Spanish-speaking pastor talking, but not one of them had ever understood what he was trying to tell them. *Now* they understood.

Day after day they arranged themselves in a circle hunched over on tiny wooden stools, carefully balancing themselves against the unevenness of the dirt floor, and read the New Testament. First one and then another would sound out the remarkable new words which spoke of Jesus Christ and His love for them—words which now sprang to their lips freely and easily.

Never before had anything held such thrilling excitement for them. All their lives they had been taught that the small brown dust-covered idols which sat so stoically in the allotted alcoves of their houses were alive and must be worshiped.

Now, through their own reading of the Word of God in their own language, they discovered for themselves that there was a true, living God and that their idols were only the work of men's hands. They discovered that the God who had made heaven and earth was inviting them as individuals to accept the salvation which He offered through a personal belief in His Son Jesus Christ! Without the aid of pastor or friend, all three cried inwardly, *"Tamastani'y, mi Christo!"* ("I will surrender my life to Christ!")

Surrender to these three joyful women meant receiving Christ as Saviour and completely obeying Him. It also involved sharing their newfound faith with their neighbors.

In their isolated village, two days' walk from the closest resemblance to modern-day civilization, three simple Totonac Indian women with resolute determination cleared the physical idols from their places of honor. Then they buried them beneath the black earth of their yards, and began answering the inquiries of their neighbors concerning the hope that had so newly sprung up within them.

The conspicuous absence of the small brown objects provoked many questions from visitors and provided all the impetus needed to start a conversion. Their joy at becoming children of God was not hid under a bushel, but was set on a hill. Now more than thirty new believers in that village have found peace with God through Christ.

Truly the gospel of Christ (in a man's own language) is the power of God unto salvation to everyone that believeth: to the Jew first, then the Greek, and also to the Totonac Indian in the jungle-covered hills of Mexico.

H.S.

13

Dorotea's Dream

DARK-HAIRED Dorotea Viniegra raced up the path to the big stone house where her "outsider" friend lived.

In keeping with the custom of her Tarahumara people who would never knock, she plopped down on a dusty boulder near the door to wait. Shortly a slim blond girl opened the door.

"Come in, Dorotea," she invited. "Mother is fixing my hair."

Dorotea crept inside the foreigner's home and saw Esther's father, Paul Carlson, working at a desk. Ramon, the thin son of the village chief, sat beside him looking at a book.

"They are putting God's words into Tarahumara so that all can understand," Esther whispered.

Dorotea feared to move closer to the missionary translator. The witch doctor had warned the villagers that evil spirits lurked around the missionary's house. But Dorotea suspected the medicine man was only jealous because the gossip was that he had once asked the missionary for some medicine for himself.

"There," Esther's mother said, "you are ready for school." Hand in hand the two girls walked outside and skipped down the steep path that led to the village schoolhouse.

The lessons were in Spanish, the official language of Mexico, but a language few of the Tarahumaras understood. Before the missionary translators came, no one had even bothered to write down the strange Tarahumara dialect. And the Tarahumaras never dreamed that there were any "outsiders" who wanted to give instead of take from them.

Esther and Dorotea became best friends. Dorotea, the shy Indian girl, found it easy to tell her blonde playmate her dearest thoughts. The two girls played together every day. They raced along the steep trails, picked flowers and berries, and waded in the cold spring-fed stream that flowed near Samachique.

As Dorotea and Esther played and studied together, the Indian girl began to doubt Tarahumara tribal beliefs and superstitions. "Don't go near still waters," the witch doctors said. "The evil spirits will make you sick." And when a village became ill, the witch doctors always blamed the sickness on the evil spirits.

Dorotea noticed that Esther's father had a medicine box full of strange-looking pills, powders, and liquids. Some of the Tarahumaras were coming to him instead of the witch doctors. Esther explained to Dorotea that illness was not caused by evil spirits, but by infection or some other natural cause. "And those who follow Jesus," Esther said, "do not need to fear the witch doctors and their evil spirits."

Often on a warm summer night Esther's father built a bonfire near the Carlson home. Tarahumara young people gathered around for games and singing. Then when the fire was dying down, Mr. Carlson talked about the true God who had revealed Himself to man. "His Son came and lived on earth long ago," Mr. Carlson said. "He died to erase the sins of all those who would believe in Him."

Sitting by Esther in the dancing shadows, Dorotea felt a stirring within her heart. She would like to believe in the true God, but wouldn't that mean betraying her people?

A great sadness came for Dorotea when Esther left to attend the "outsiders'" high school in far-off California. When the Carlsons prepared to take a year's furlough, Dorotea asked her father for permission to join Esther in the outsiders' school.

"No one from our people has ever gone to the outsiders' school," her father said. "Why do you wish to be the first?"

Tears brimmed in Dorotea's eyes as she explained her longing to help her people. Her father gave his consent.

Dorotea was eighteen when she enrolled in the senior class of Grossman High School near San Diego. She studied English while the other students took Spanish lessons. Her grades surprised the students and faculty, although with only one year of credits she could not graduate with the class.

Before returning to the Tarahumara tribe with the Carlsons, Dorotea announced that she had become a believer in Christ. "I love my people," she said, "but I can no longer follow the old customs. I must follow Christ."

Back in Mexico, Dorotea applied to the Methodist nursing school in her state capital, Chihuahua City. The director accepted her with doubts because Dorotea did not have a high school diploma.

However, the Indian girl became one of the school's best students and was elected "outstanding student nurse in surgical nursing." When she finished her training, she was appointed director of nurses at a hospital in Cuauhtémoc, Mexico. Today she works in a government clinic that serves the Tarahumaras and other Indian groups.

Recently a Mexican social worker visited the Carlsons in Samachique. "I work with Dorotea," she said. "We have known many people who talked about Christianity, but until Dorotea came we never knew one who really lives her faith."

J.C.H.

6-400

J